Hortense Ullrich

Never Kiss a Witch

Aus dem Deutschen
von Philip und Regine Hewitt

Thienemann

Sunday, 5th April

A diary! Wow! How did I ever **get on** without one!

"Dear Josefine, my diary was my most important companion in those far-off days when I was a teenager," is what my aunt wrote about the empty book she sent me.

But a diary, **of all things**. Well, I suppose it's a **teeny-weeny bit** better than the terrible pyjamas she normally sends. She managed to jump from baby design – little teddy bears and pussy cats – to granny-type monstrosities with flowery patterns without ever sending a pair of pyjamas that might have suited my taste.

And my mother is always delighted. "Well, Jojo," she says, "that really is something nice! I didn't know they still made things like that nowadays!" Makes you think, doesn't it?

And now a diary.

Whoever keeps a diary in the computer age? You won't find diaries in **bedside cabinet drawers** any

---

to get on – auskommen; of all things – ausgerechnet; teeny-weeny bit – ein klitzekleines bisschen

more. In any case, when was the last time you saw a bedside cabinet drawer?

At least **nosey** mums no longer **poke around** their daughters' bedrooms looking for diaries. They look for diskettes with secret notes. That's why passwords were invented. Because in the meantime more and more parents seem to have acquired quite astonishing computer skills. Some of them have even got beyond switching the thing on, and there are rumours that, while we are **unsuspectingly** learning for life at school, our parents are sitting in front of the computer at home playing precisely those games that they are constantly forbidding us. Never mind.

What am I supposed to do with a diary!?

"You can trust your diary to keep secrets no one else should know," she writes.

In my life there are no things which no one else should know.

My life is an open book. Or, to put it differently, an empty book.

My life is as boring as hell.

I've got the most **nerve-racking** little sister in the world, the most disorganized mother in the world and the most stupid female classmates in the world.

---

bedside cabinet drawer – Nachttischschublade;
nosey – neugierig; to poke around – herumstöbern;
unsuspectingly – ahnungslos; nerve-racking – nervtötend

And I don't mind anyone knowing it. So what do I need a diary for?

But it wasn't always like that. What I said about my sister and my mum still is the same, but at school things were quite different until **recently**.

And it's all that stupid Serafina's fault that things are now no longer what they used to be. It was she who divided us up into 'cool' and 'uncool' kids. And where did she put me? In the uncool category!

Until then, cool or uncool had not been a big **issue**. Some people were OK; others were a bit **screwy**, but somehow I managed to get on with everyone. And now this.

Suddenly I'm uncool and sit around alone at home in the afternoons. I can't understand it.

Everything was fine until this **snake-in-the-grass** Serafina turned up. Linda, Isabell, Julia and I always met after school. Sometimes other girls came along, sometimes boys from our class. We never made any firm plans. We went off on our bikes or our roller-blades or went down to the riding stables to see the horses. Everything was **hunky-dory**.

Then a new girl joined our class: Serafina.

First she asked politely whether she could come with us, and we said yes. No prob. Why not? After

---

recently – vor kurzem; issue – Thema; screwy – verdreht; snake-in-the-grass – falsche Schlange; hunky-dory – in Butter all, we're nice kids. Unlike Serafina. First she **pretended** to find everything fantastic. Especially the horses. Then she began, gradually and **hypocritically**, to explain to us that we were living right on the **dark side of the moon**.

No thirteen-year-old, she said, still read magazines about horses, or comics. We could, after all, get magazines for teenagers. And it was no longer the 'in' thing to put up posters of horses in your bedroom. Posters of cool singers, actors and actresses. And the hot topic at our age, she told us, was not **plaiting** friendship bracelets but BOYS. Boys of the right kind, of course. They had to be at least fifteen. There could be no question of hanging around with boys from our class. They were all still small children. We would simply be **making fools of ourselves**.

We listened to what she said with interest.

Hey! Why not? You're never too young to learn. So Serafina introduced us to the big wide world of cool kids as well as giving us tips on make-up and **gear**.

I thought she was going a bit far for a newcomer and told her that **we had got along** quite well so far without her advice.

---

to pretend – so tun, als ob; hypocritically – scheinheilig; dark side of the moon – hinterm Mond; to plait – flechten; to make a fool of oneself – sich zum Narren machen; gear – Klamotten; to get along – klarkommen

Serafina took it all with a **supercilious** smile. But then she made ready for the decisive blow. So skilfully that no one noticed what was really happening.

Suddenly Serafina became the **spokesperson** of our little afternoon group, saying that we couldn't allow just anyone to hang around with us. She was now going to start a club to which only cool girls could belong. I thought that was a bit of a **dotty** idea, but I was convinced that she thought that girls like Andrea, Gudrun and Sophie-Marie were uncool. I was right. She did. And she excluded them right from the start. But she did the same to me!

Her criterion for acceptance was the following: she asked us who we were in love with. "Nobody" I said without hesitation. First of all, it's true, secondly, if I were in love with anyone, Serafina is certainly the last person I'd tell. I think boys are stupid, anyway.

That was the end of any idea of being a member of the club. Because Serafina said that anyone who wasn't in love was definitely still a baby and not acceptable for her club.

Then she asked Julia, Linda and Isabell. They were cleverer. They didn't want to make my mistake, so they began by cautiously asking who Serafina thought was great.

---

supercilious – hochnäsig; spokesperson – Wortführerin; dotty – verrückt

Serafina said that was **clear as crystal**: there was only one cool boy at our school – BJ, the singer in our school band.

He's fifteen and in Ninth **Grade**. His real name is Bernd-Jens, but he won't let anyone call him that. Not even our teachers. He's crazy about America and insists on the American pronunciation of his two initials. None of us would have had the idea of falling in love with BJ.

But my ex-friends suddenly chorused: Yes, they thought he was fantastic – they'd all been in love with him for ages.

Serafina nodded with satisfaction and then said to the other uncool girls – myself included – that the club was now complete. We could found our own club if we wanted.

"A horse-lovers' club, maybe," she said. But that sounded neither comradely nor encouraging.

I said I thought that clubs were stupid anyway.

Serafina shrugged her shoulders and said **cheekily**: "Whatever you say." She **linked** my friends and marched off with them.

Great! My life is not only as boring as hell, it's over now.

But at least I have a diary. Ha ha ha!

---

clear as crystal – klar wie Kloßbrühe; Grade – Jahrgangsstufe; cheekily – schnippisch; to link sb – jmd. unterhaken

Monday, 6th April

Linda came round to see me again yesterday evening. Secretly, of course, so that Serafina won't find out. Because Linda is frightened of being kicked out of the club if she talks to uncool kids.

And Linda begged me to make an effort to become a bit cooler. She said I shouldn't **make such a fuss** and please would I fall in love with BJ immediately. When Serafina notices that, she surely will offer to let me become a member of her club.

Linda is missing me, of course. She thinks it would be more fun for her if I were also a member of the club.

I'll think about it.

Maybe I'll do Linda that favour.

Tuesday, 7th April

I've made up my mind now.

I'll fall in love with BJ, too. I'm only doing it for Linda's sake, of course. Not because of Serafina's stupid club. Because her club is actually a kind of BJ-Serafina Fan Club. If you don't **rave about** BJ all the time, Serafina **puts the pressure on**.

---

to make a fuss – sich anstellen; rave about sb – für jmd. schwärmen; to put the pressure on – Stress machen

Linda once said that she thought Patrick was great. Serafina immediately made fun of Linda. Then Linda told her she was only joking and that she was in love with BJ, too. Then Serafina said she was pleased to hear it, for she would certainly have missed Linda as a member of the club.

Another time Linda said that she thought Justus was great. Serafina said that was out of the question. Justus was her brother. Linda had to stick to the rules of the club.

Another rule says that you must always listen attentively to Serafina. Because she lectures her fans all break long on how life works. And in the afternoons she questions them on how much they remember. Seriously! I could hardly believe it. In order to be a member of Serafina's club you have to do homework that Serafina sets you. Yesterday Isabell didn't know straight off how to produce a wet-look hairstyle (she had mixed up gel and spray), and Serafina gave her a written warning! Isabell started crying, and it took Linda a long time to calm her down.

Serafina has got **autographs** from every important band, knows what the stars eat for breakfast, where they spend their holidays and who **is in whose hair** at this very moment in time. She knows how you have to dress in order to **win over** male film

---

autograph – Autogramm; to be in sbs hair – mit jmd. Zoff haben; to win over sb – jmd. erobern

stars, how to break their hearts and how you have to style your hair to make boys over fifteen fall in love with you.

In a word, Serafina is cool. She says so herself, and in the meantime the other girls in her club say so, too, hoping, of course, that some of Serafina's coolness will **rub off** on them.

I could use a bit of coolness myself. This deficit is all my mother's fault. She regularly makes sure that people notice how totally uncool I am.

She's always running after me with my umbrella and my **wellies** – sometimes all the way to school! And in winter she comes trotting along with my scarf and cap.

She could never imagine that I have good reasons for wanting to 'forget' these embarrassing things.

But even all that wouldn't be too bad. The problem is the way she does it. Normal mothers would just hang whatever it was on the clothes **pegs** outside the classroom. Not my mother. She comes into the classroom every time – during the lessons! And the way she does it! She tiptoes **conspicuously** in, making as much noise as possible. The first time most of the class took her for an extremely untal-

---

to rub off – abfärben; wellies – Gummistiefel; peg – Haken; conspicuously – auffällig

ented burglar. In the meantime, some of them even call out: “Hello, Mrs Sonntag!” when she comes creeping in.

If the teachers stop what they’re doing, she simply raises her hand and says in a loud whisper: “Don’t let me interrupt you. Just pretend I’m not there. I’ll be gone in a moment.”

Then she comes over to me and whispers at about 130 decibels, gives me a big cuddle as if we weren’t going to see each other for six months and creeps out of the room, stumbling over at least three **satchels**.

At the door she turns round again and blows me kisses until the teachers ask whether everything is OK or not.

My mother nods eagerly. “Oh yes! Everything’s OK. The child just forgot her wellies. Don’t let me disturb you, I’m leaving now.”

Then she opens the door the wrong way round. She pushes the handle downwards, which opens the door slightly. Then she pulls it instead of pushing. The door slams shut. Then she turns round, smiling guiltily, and whispers: “**Panic door**, of course – opens outwards. I keep forgetting.” After that she finally leaves, having **embarrassed** me **into the ground**. The teachers have decided in the

---

satchel – Schultasche; panic door – Fluchttür;
embarrassed to the ground – bis auf die Knochen blamiert

meantime to fix a 'push' sign to the door. Especially for my mother.

A few weeks later, when most of the class have forgotten my mother's performance and are just beginning to stop teasing me about it, she pokes her head round the door again and the whole nonsense is repeated.

But seriously – who in the world would **stage an act** like that? Only someone who wants to destroy her daughter socially.

Friday, 10th April

I've already been in love with BJ for three days, and it's working out quite well. Whenever I see him, I blink my eyes and sigh a little if Serafina is nearby.

But Serafina still hasn't offered me membership in her club. She only says: "Forget him, Baby!"

I don't know what she means. Is it some kind of membership test for the club?

I told her: "I can fall in love with whomever I want!"

I thought that sounded quite cool.

---

to stage an act – eine Nummer abziehen

Monday, 13th April

I hate Serafina.

She told BJ that I was in love with him. What a nasty thing to do!

And Serafina said he told her not to bother him with such kiddie stuff. He said he didn't even know who Jojo was!

Very embarrassing.

Then Serafina told me that she didn't think it was a good idea for people to see me and her together. She said she was worried about her **reputation**. She would lose it because I wasn't cool enough.

What a stupid, **conceited toad**! Thinks she's super-duper cool! **PUKE**! Innocently **twittering** away and flashing her mascara-ed eyelashes! Yes indeed – mascara-ed. She has more different shades of mascara in her school bag than coloured pencils.

And when she wants something from you, she pretends to be as sweet as sugar-candy. A diabetic would collapse in a coma.

Not even our teachers can see through her performance. Trained educationalists – bah! It's so easy **to pull the wool over their eyes**. When they're

---

reputation – guter Ruf; conceited toad – eingebildete Kröte; Puke! – Kotz!; to twitter – zwitschern, flöten; to pull the wool over sb's eyes – jmd. hinters Licht führen

not looking, **she has a go at anyone** who isn't a member of her fan club. She is mean and two-faced. And everyone **puts up with** it.

Someone really ought to do something.

Tuesday, 14th April

Today she started sitting next to me in class.

She got round our **form mistress** by looking at her with upcast, **beseeching** eyes.

Actually Serafina thinks it's below her dignity to sit next to anyone who doesn't know how to put basic make-up tips into practice. But because she's **as thick as two short planks**, she needs someone she can copy off. Because the chickens – I mean her girl-friends of course, but because they're always **cackling** about something and **clucking to one another**, I shall refer to them as chickens from now on – they also have brains about the size of a hen's. That's why Serafina chose me. Nobody is better than me at maths. And Mr Baumann has told Serafina that if she doesn't do bet-

---

to have a go at sb – auf jmd. losgehen; to put up with sth – sich etwas gefallen lassen; form mistress – Klassenlehrerin; beseeching – flehentlich; as thick as two short planks – strohdoof; to cackle – gackern; to cluck to one another – zusammenglucken

ter work in maths, the outlook will be black for her.

So she immediately started **buttering me up**. And she's even invited me to her birthday party.

"Jojo, my dear. What would I do without you!" she always says in a very theatrical voice (she watches too many soap operas) as she takes my maths exercise book and copies out the answers. I don't care. It leaves me completely cool.

Thursday, 16th April

I shouldn't have gone to Serafina's birthday party.

And above all I shouldn't have listened to my mother. "Paint her a picture, Jojo darling."

I hate it when she says that to me. I'm thirteen, for Christ's sake, and not her darling any more.

"A picture is something personal, and you're so good at painting. She likes horses, doesn't she? You used to go to the stables with her a lot."

So, without thinking any more about it, idiotically I painted a Lippizano horse from one of my horse posters – Serafina's favourite horse. At least that's what she told me at the time. It was a really **smashing** painting. Honestly.

---

to butter sb up – sich bei jmd. einschleimen; smashing – toll

But Serafina didn't think so, and pulled a face. How embarrassing. In front of all the others.

She smiled a silly smile and said in her sweet-as-sugar voice: "So, you're still only thinking about horses, are you?" Then she gave the other chickens a knowing look and, picking up my painting between the tips of finger and thumb, deposited it on the pile of used wrapping paper.

The chickens made cackling noises, and I thought I would die.

I'm so stupid. I should have known that would happen.

But it's really all my mother's fault. How can she advise her thirteen-year-old daughter that painting a picture is a suitable birthday present for a cool teenager? What a stupid idea!

If my mother hadn't stopped my pocket-money, I could have given Serafina a CD. But no, last week she had another **attack** of 'how to bring up children' and thought she would have to teach me a lesson.

Just because I mixed up the stupid costumes.

It's like this, you see: my mother works at the theatre. She rang up from there in a panic and in a hectic mood as always – she was born like that: absent-minded, never in control of the situation. "Jojo, darling. You have to do me a favour. Bring the

---

attack – Anfall

witch's costume to the children's theatre as quick as you can. I left it at home. The performance is due to start soon."

So it should be clear that it was she who **had screwed the whole thing up**. But never mind.

I did exactly what she told me, but must have grabbed the wrong costume. A natural mistake. So the Witch in Hansel and Gretel emerged from her cottage in a rococo costume. Everyone roared with laughter. I thought it livened up the performance a **treat**.

But my mother didn't think so. She was convinced I'd done it **deliberately**. She said that she thought someone of my age ought to be able to distinguish a rococo costume from a witch's costume.

I thought the witch's costume looked a bit worn and **tatty**. The other costume looked much better. How could I know that theatre people are so narrow-minded?

Anyway, my mother got into trouble over it. And so, of course, did I.

My mother designs and **sews** costumes for the theatre. Here at home.

Why can't she work in an office all day like all

---

to screw sth up – etw. vermasseln; treat – Vergnügen; deliberately – absichtlich; tatty – zerlumpt; to sew – nähen

other normal mothers? It's obvious: because she isn't normal. Nothing in our family is done like it is in other families. Regular meals and home cooking are things which I've only ever seen on TV.

My mother is completely chaotic and always completely surprised when I say: "I'm hungry."

"What, again?" she says in shocked tones. "You've only just eaten!"

OK, that was seven hours ago. A bowl of cornflakes for breakfast.

I owe my survival to the invention of the microwave oven, because my mother still hasn't worked out why there is a kitchen in our flat. She sews fantastic costumes but doesn't know how to prepare scrambled eggs.

But that has its good side, too. She actually believes that a **jelly-baby** sandwich contains **bags of** vitamins simply because I told her that the colours are produced from fruit juices. So in our family, jelly-babies count as fruit.

And one thing is clear – she **dotes on me**. She would do anything for me, and her only goal in life is to make me happy.

Unless of course she has just finished reading one of her brilliant 'bringing-up children' books. Then she tries to be as **strict** as possible. She runs

---

jelly-baby – Gummibärchen; bags of – jede Menge;
to dote on sb – jmd. über alles lieben; strict – streng

around the flat looking for objects on which to try out her latest upbringing theories.

"Josefine, you haven't done your homework yet. Switch that TV off immediately!"

Then, when I accept my fate and creep out of the living-room with my head hung low, she runs after me and says: "I'm sorry, darling, I didn't mean it like that. But you have to understand …"

I reply: "Of course, Mummy, you're absolutely right."

The fact that I am being **sensible** and say that she is right completely **knocks the stuffing out of her**, and she tells me to finish watching the programme and do my homework afterwards.

I say 'No'.

She **insists**.

And if I play my cards right, she is begging me to watch music videos for half an hour after my favourite programme has finished. I do what she tells me, like a good little girl, and she is very proud of the way she is bringing me up. She has, of course, completely forgotten the matter of my homework.

But that's not bad, because she has no idea of what goes on at school anyway.

At the last **PTA meeting**, she spent the evening in the wrong classroom. In Grade 6.

---

sensible – vernünftig; to knock the stuffing out of sb – jmd. fertig machen; to insist – auf etw. bestehen; PTA meeting – Elternabend

When she said goodbye to the teacher and told her I hadn't said that I had a new form mistress, she smiled at my mother coldly and said: "Mrs Sonntag, your daughter Josefine is not in my form. Not even in this Grade. She's in Grade 7 already."

And instead of being embarrassed, my mother simply said, in a surprised voice: "Really? My goodness! How time flies!"

That's my mother. A hopeless case.

Anyway, she found a job where she can work from home, thus **spoiling** all my afternoons. And she even has an educational explanation ready: "Children ought to feel that their mothers are always there for them."

That's what's called compensation. She has a bad conscience because her husband ran off leaving her with two small kids. Hey, what's so abnormal about that? I don't know a single family still **starring the original cast**.

Well, with the exception of Serafina's. The Meiers live the kind of life you see in trashy films. Peace, harmony and joy. The father is still living with them. But only because he is frightened of his wife. She would never allow him **to sling his hook**. But then she's a real **bitch**. Just like her daughter.

---

to spoil – verpatzen; starring the original cast – in der Originalbesetzung spielen; to sling his hook – die Fliege machen; bitch – Zicke

Only their son is different. Justus is quite OK. Justus is fifteen. And Justus is in the same form as BJ. I'm sure that Serafina has forced her brother to make friends with BJ to improve her chances.

The longer I pretend to be in love with BJ, the better it works. BJ is so-o-o-o sweet. How come I never noticed it before? He's got his own band and they have plenty of **gigs**. That's why so many girls are in love with him. Especially Serafina. She thinks **she's entitled** to BJ because she thinks she's the most beautiful girl. She wants to be a model, and believes that musicians only ever marry models. You only have to read the right magazines to realize what goes on in the world, she says.

And of course BJ witnessed the entire **embarrassing** episode with my horse picture. He was at Serafina's party. Although he didn't want to come. Serafina is so clever.

Serafina had invited BJ and a couple of the boys from his band to her birthday party, but they **turned** the invitation **down**.

So Serafina changed the date of her party to precisely the day on which Justus had invited BJ to their flat.

At first Serafina pretended to be very surprised,

---

gig – Auftritt; to be entitled – einen Anspruch haben; embarrassing – peinlich; to turn down – absagen in the manner of 'what a **coincidence**!' Then she pretended to be **flattered** that BJ had come to her birthday party specially. And finally she managed to persuade him to sing a song for her. The chickens could hardly move for love and admiration. I was so annoyed with Serafina that I almost forgot I was in love with BJ, too.

Since the silly geese laughed at my hand-painted horse picture, of course, my chances are ruined. Because BJ witnessed the whole thing. Now he'll never think I'm cool.

It was then that Justus **interfered**. He fished out my painting from the pile of wrapping paper, looked at it with expert eye and said he had found the **fitting instructions** for a washing machine. Was anybody missing them? I had to laugh myself. Justus is really funny.

But then he said quietly to me: "I think it's really good. You've got a talent."

What good is that to me if BJ doesn't think I'm cool?

Serafina is lucky.

Lucky even to have a big brother like that. She's always got plenty of boys in her flat. And that's the reason why Serafina has such a **gaggle** of silly chickens always cackling around her, because she

---

coincidence – Zufall; flattered – geschmeichelt;
to interfere – sich einmischen; fitting instructions – Bauplan; gaggle – Schar

promises them that they can **get a glimpse** of her big brother and his mates.

Sometimes she even persuades her brother to take her and the chickens to the cinema with him. I really can't imagine how she does it. She probably **blackmails** him. Because Justus is really too nice to be hanging around with his brainless sister all the time.

But you mustn't think I **have a crush on** Justus.

Actually, I think all boys are stupid. Even BJ is stupid somehow. Mr Supercool. But he does have a band of his own.

I'll really have to get BJ to fall in love with *me.* Then Serafina will explode with **jealousy**. And that would be the only **just** punishment for her.

Friday, 17th April

Today he **bumped into me**. Linda thinks he nearly knocked me over simply because he didn't see me. But I don't believe her. It was definitely an

---

to get a glimpse – einen Blick werfen; to blackmail – erpressen; to have a crush on sb – in jmd. verknallt sein; jealousy – Eifersucht; just – gerecht; to bump into sb – mit jmd. zusammenstoßen

advance – an attempt to get closer to me. Boys are sometimes very shy, and this is their way of showing their love for a girl.

Quite apart from that, the **bruise** on my knee has the shape of a heart. If that isn't a clear symbol!

My head is still going round and round. So I'm suffering either from concussion or puberty.

My mother keeps **babbling** on about me having reached puberty and that the strangest things happen then. That is, she says, something quite normal and natural. But what an **anticlimax**. Nothing happens. I still haven't got any breasts and not even a single **pimple**. I think that's the least you can expect of puberty. One tiny pimple. Then the others will at least see that you're now grown up. Never mind.

Shit. Now my mother's grumbling at me again. She wants me to switch off the light and get into bed. She thinks I need rest **badly**.

---

advance – Annäherungsversuch; bruise – blauer Fleck; to babble – quasseln; anticlimax – Enttäuschung; pimple – Pickel; badly – dringend

Saturday morning, 18th April

I hate Flippi.

Such a annoying little **tick**. Little sisters are a real punishment. How can parents possibly imagine that you would want a little sister? Absolute nonsense!

I distinctly told them at the time: I want either a big brother or a dog.

No deal. What do I get? A sister five years younger than me. What good is that to me?

My mother realized that later. Even with one child she was often **at the end of her tether**: "The child has far too much imagination and wastes it all on nonsense."

Then she gave birth to Flippi. Her real name is Filipine. My mother obviously has a problem with names. Be honest: who with any sense would call her daughters Josefine and Filipine?

Only someone herself called Isolde! If her intention was to pass the name **curse** on to us, she certainly succeeded.

Whenever Flippi **gets into mischief** she always sighs: "Flippi is the boy I never wanted."

Flippi breeds snails and loves all disgusting

---

tick – Zecke; to be at the end of one's tether – am Ende seiner Kräfte sein; curse – Fluch; to get into mischief – etwas anstellen

things. I think she selects her favourite animals in accordance with the '**Yuck**!' factor. The more people say 'Yuck!' to a creature, the more she likes it.

So we have progressed from a collection of **wood-lice** via an **earthworm** breeding station to a colony of spiders.

At present, it's snails. But not the nice ones with shells. She started off with them, but my mother made the mistake of saying: "Oh! They look quite nice." So Flippi immediately switched to **slugs**.

It's all my mother's fault. I told her at the time I'd rather have a dog than a sister. She'd be better off with a dog. And so would I.

But I was going to tell you about my day. It began like this: I was lying in bed with the best dream of the century: I am in the park with BJ. He is about to kiss me when, suddenly, my mouth is full of the most disgusting thing I've ever tasted: shower gel. I wake up in shock and what do I find – shower gel in my mouth. Honestly.

Stupid Flippi had emptied the tube into my mouth. She said I had opened my mouth in such a gesture of desire that she couldn't resist. What was the **skunk** doing in my bedroom anyway? Especially when I was asleep.

---

yuck – igitt; wood-lice – Kellerasseln; earthworm – Regenwurm; slug – Nacktschnecke; skunk – Stinktier

I was absolutely **livid**. I threw my pillow at her, jumped on top of her and tried to **throttle** her.

Flippi leapt forwards and kicked me in the stomach. I fell back into my bookshelves and was almost buried under down-falling books.

At that moment, of course, my mother came into the room. She stared at me, turned her eyes heavenwards and simply said: "Josefine" (whenever she says Josefine she is either at a complete loss or very, very angry). "Josefine," she said. "I don't want to know what's going on here. But whatever it is, put it right immediately – and I mean immediately."

She grabbed Flippi, dragged her out of the room and slammed the door behind her.

Can't this woman put two and two together? I mean, the situation is quite plain: she finds Flippi in my room – a clear case of **trespassing** on private property. I could have called the police. My mother never draws the right conclusions.

All she can think of is making me responsible for clearing up the mess.

Why does she never try to find out which person is really guilty? She always **grumbles at** me. Only at me. If I'm very lucky, she sometimes screams in the plural. But I'm sure it's only to give me the impression that she is also shouting at Flippi.

---

livid – stinksauer; to throttle – erwürgen; trespassing – unbefugtes Betreten; to grumble at sb – an jmd. rummeckern

I'm sure she takes Flippi aside later on and apologizes for having had to talk so loud, hoping that she hasn't hurt Flippi's tender little ears and saying that she is, of course, never angry with Flippi, only with me. **Bet you** I'm right **on all counts**!

The longer I thought about it, the angrier I got. I got so angry that I kicked my wastepaper basket. It went sailing towards my bedroom door just as my mother was coming back in. She probably only wanted to say something, but she caught the wastepaper basket in a reflex action and stared very **reproachfully** at me. Not even a **snippet** had fallen on the floor. The basket was still full of rubbish.

Flippi had slipped back into my room and **made a rush at me**. And before I could say 'knife', the little **poisoned dwarf** had boxed my ears and kicked me on the **shin**.

I was **seething with anger** by this time. I looked around and saw a big, fat volume of my encyclopaedia right in front of me. I picked it up in both hands and raised it above my head. My mother saw what I was doing and roused herself from her **lethargy**. I was just about to crash the encyclopaedia down on Flippi's head when my mother upturned

---

bet you – wetten, dass; on all counts – hundertprozentig; reproachfully – vorwurfsvoll; snippet – Schnipsel; to make a rush at sb – sich auf jmd. stürzen; poisoned dwarf – Giftzwerg; shin – Schienbein; to seeth with anger – vor Wut kochen; lethargy – Erstarrung

the wastepaper basket over Flippi's head like a kind of safety helmet. I'm sure she really only meant to protect her favourite, and in her state of shock this was the only thing she could think of doing. It was an obvious reaction. But somehow it did not make a very motherly impression. Any my floor is now covered in rubbish.

Flippi, at least, began to howl. More out of **fright**, for she had no idea what was happening to her. My mother was standing behind her and Flippi hadn't seen the wastepaper basket. She almost certainly thought I had hit her, because she began screaming hysterically: "Help! Help! I'm blind, I can't see anything! Jojo hit me on the head and now I'm blind! Help, Mummy!"

I thought that as Flippi was screaming, I'd better do some screaming of my own. I don't know what I said, but I'm sure it didn't do much to calm Flippi down.

That was too much for my mother. She **flipped her lid**. She freed Flippi from the wastepaper basket and ordered both of us to stay in our rooms until further notice.

As a punishment, we're not allowed to go to the theatre with her to see the costumes being tried on. A punishment? Don't make me laugh! Anyway, I've got more important things to do.

---

fright – Schreck; to flip one's lid – ausrasten

But to be on the safe side I **sobbed** a little and then **groaned** a little to myself about how untidy my room now looked before kneeling down **meekly** on the floor to collect the contents of my wastepaper basket again. Then I sobbed a little more.

My mother then immediately gives up and is sorry for everything. I should have remembered that. Because the next thing she said was: "All right, you can come with me **after all**."

I could have kicked myself! I told her 'no' and said I wanted to be punished. It was OK – I deserved it. I told her just to take Flippi with her. (Because I thought that Flippi deserved this punishment.)

My mother was quite **repentant** but I insisted. So she trotted off with Flippi (grumbling as usual).

It was only then that I was able to try and rinse the shower gel out of my mouth. But it didn't work. I gargled soap bubbles. When I talked, I foamed at the mouth. And I couldn't **get rid of** the taste, either. I **cursed and swore**.

In America, apparently, mothers wash their children's mouths out with soap if they use naughty words. All I can say is that the best **swearwords** only come when you have the taste of soap in your mouth.

---

to sob – schluchzen; to groan – jammern; meekly – demütig; after all – trotzdem; repentant – reumütig; to get rid of sth – etwas loswerden; to curse and swear – schimpfen und fluchen; swearwords – Schimpfwörter

Saturday evening, 18th April

But that was only the beginning.

I was sitting on my bed wondering what to do. I tried out a couple of hair styles, **dyed** a few **strands** of hair pink and blue, and practised kissing in front of the mirror.

Then I cleaned the mirror again and emptied my jacket pockets. I found a lot of junk in them: three marbles, a pencil sharpener shaped like a cowboy hat, two neon elastic hair bands, a dried-out slug which had probably fled from Flippi and found **refuge** in my pocket, and half a hot dog from Serafina's birthday party.

Inside the hot dog I suddenly found Serafina's golden chain that her **godmother** had given her for her birthday.

No idea how the chain found its way into my hot dog.

It could only have happened when one of my hot dogs fell onto the table with the presents. I had grabbed myself three hot dogs because I love hot dogs and was worried that there might not be enough. I was standing in front of the table with three hot dogs in my hands, looking at Serafina's presents. One of the sausages slipped out of the

---

to dye – färben; strand – Strähne; refuge – Zuflucht; godmother – Patentante

roll and landed on Serafina's gift table. I tried to scoop up the sausage but didn't want to get my fingers dirty, so I chased it with the roll. What I mean is that I kept on opening and closing the roll over the sausage, but it skidded away across the table leaving a rather ugly trail of ketchup on the presents.

And while this was going on, the sausage must somehow have **hooked onto** the chain without me noticing.

But how did it find its way into my jacket pocket? Now I remember: because of BJ. Serafina's party had suddenly become a **bit of a bore**. Justus and BJ left, Serafina was still angry with me, and the chickens began to tell Serafina how wonderful and how charming she was. I would have **thrown up** if I'd had to listen to that for much longer, so I went off home with my two remaining hot dogs.

I had already eaten one when I saw BJ and Justus standing outside the ice-cream parlour.

I immediately slipped the other hot dog into my jacket pocket. I thought that BJ might want to speak to me. We might get into conversation and talk and talk. It might be a bad idea to be eating a hot dog at the time.

But nothing of the sort happened. BJ didn't even

---

to hook onto – sich verheddern; bit of a bore – ziemlich langweilig; to throw up – sich übergeben

see me, and Justus only waved briefly. This did nothing to improve my bad mood and I didn't feel hungry any more. Quite apart from which, I had forgotten all about the hot dog.

So there I stood in my room this morning with the old hot dog and the gold chain in my hand, wondering what would be the best thing to do about it.

I've got a special BJ **scrapbook** into which I stick anything to do with BJ. That's what people do when they are in love with film or pop stars. And I was just wondering whether to stick the hot dog in, and what would be the best way to flatten it first (the **desiccated** slug would have slipped in easily, maybe I'll use that) when the doorbell rang.

Still holding the gold necklace and the hot dog, I went to the door and opened it. It was Linda, and her eyes opened as wide as teacups when she saw the gold chain.

"Oh dear! I don't believe it!" exclaimed Linda. "Jojo! How could you?"

This annoyed me. What sort of a greeting was that?

"What's the matter?" I **snapped**. "**Talk sense**."

Linda pointed to the chain. "You **nicked** Serafina's gold necklace!"

---

scrapbook – Sammelalbum; desiccated – ausgetrocknet; to snap – jmd. anschnauzen; to talk sense – Klartext reden; to nick – klauen

"Nonsense! Of course I didn't. It was in my hot dog."

"Oh dear! I've just been round at Serafina's. She's absolutely furious. Her mother wants to call the police."

I suddenly felt sick by fear. If I go to prison, BJ will certainly never have anything to do with me. That will be the end of our romance, and there will be no obstacles in Serafina's path.

Without thinking twice, Linda **dragged** me outside. "Come on. Let's go round to her place quick. You can give her the necklace back and say it was all a mistake."

Panic-stricken, I ran after her.

Soon afterwards we were standing outside Serafina's front door. I looked down at my feet and thought I would die. In my panic I had completely forgotten to get dressed. I was standing there in my pyjamas. The pair covered in miniature pandas, of course! From my godmother: the one who sent me all those terrible pairs of pyjamas and this diary!

I felt embarrassed to death, standing there outside Serafina's front door, but Linda calmly rang the bell and waited until Serafina **poked her head round the door**.

---

to drag – zerren; to poke one's head around the door – den Kopf zur Tür rausstrecken

When she saw me, she raised her eyebrows and asked. "What are you doing here?"

I could hardly believe it. First she invites me to her birthday party, then, two days later, she behaves as if it were the height of **impertinence** to ring her doorbell.

Well, perhaps it was the ketchup **stains**. But they really weren't my fault.

When I wanted to put ketchup on my hot dog at her party, the bottle somehow slipped, somehow **disgorging** a large **splodge** across Serafina's new silk blouse. Was she angry! And so was her mother. They both **squealed** as if I had sat down on the birthday cake.

All I said was: "It'll wash out with plain water. It's only cheap ketchup. It won't leave a stain."

Somehow that didn't pacify them, and Serafina began to yell even louder that I had done it **on purpose,** etc.

Well, honestly, I was quite surprised how much came out. I thought it would only be a little **squirt**, and you would hardly have seen that on the blouse.

Serafina had to put a new blouse on. She ordered me not to come anywhere near her. That's

---

impertinence – Unverschämtheit; stain – Fleck;
to disgorge – ausspucken; splodge – Schwall; to squeal – kreischen; on purpose – mit Absicht; squirt – Spritzer

why I got up and went to look at the presents. Then the sausage fell out of my hot dog onto the table, and that's when I must have picked up the necklace. So everything is really Serafina's fault, you see.

So there I was, standing stupidly outside Serafina's front door with the hot-dog necklace in one hand, saying: "I've found something. I think it belongs to you." I held out the necklace.

She **tore** it out of my hand and slammed the door. **How about that**!

I was alone again with Linda outside Serafina's front door. Me in my pyjamas. The pyjamas with the pandas on them.

It was just at that moment that Justus came round the corner. The **twit** looked me up and down.

"Sexy outfit, Jojo." He grinned.

I just said "Idiot" and moved away from him as quickly as I could. Stupidly enough, I **blushed**. I never blush normally.

Only sometimes, when this stupid Justus is around. And I don't even **fancy** him. Honestly.

I then marched Linda off to the park and **gave her a piece of my mind**. How could she drag me

---

to tear – reißen; How about that? – Wie findet man das?; twit – Knallkopf; to blush – rot werden; to fancy sb – auf jmd. stehen; to give sb a piece of one's mind – jmd. die Meinung sagen

out of my flat in my pyjamas. What a rotten thing to do!

Unfortunately, my maths teacher happened to walk by at that very moment. He stared at me, came closer and asked if everything was OK.

I really couldn't think what to say. I pretended to be a sleepwalker and marched off with my arms stretched out in front of me. It was convincing enough, because I was still wearing my pyjamas, of course. When I was out of sight, I began walking a little faster and **rushed** back home.

I hope Justus won't tell BJ about my pyjama performance. That would be too embarrassing for words!

Sunday, 19th April

The necklace incident still makes me **feel queasy**. **Missing** jail **by inches**!

Serafina really is lucky. She has a big brother, all my girl-friends and even gets wonderful birthday presents. Serafina's godmother **solemnly** presented

---

to rush – rasen; to feel queasy – Übelkeit empfinden; missing sth by inches – knapp an etwas vorbei; solemnly – feierlich

her with the necklace, and Serafina's mother announced to all of us that, from now on, Serafina will get a gold heart set with a precious stone to hang on the necklace every year. Until she's eighteen. Although I thought it was intolerably **swanky**, it's really a super idea.

My mother would never think up an idea like that. As a thirteenth-birthday present, she just enrolled me in some stupid book club. I'll now be getting a twenty-four-volume encyclopaedia from them. One volume per month. **Big deal**! Just what a girl of my age would have wanted!

I envy Serafina. Not only because of the necklace and her godmother. Also because of Justus.

I don't really envy her because of Justus. But he is BJ's best friend. So she always gets the latest BJ stories. And when BJ comes to see her brother, they're even in the same flat. She can touch the **door handle** after BJ has touched it, or drink out of his glass when he's gone. Sometimes, when the boys are hanging around the flat, Serafina can be the **referee** when the boys see who can **burp** the loudest. She always lets BJ win, of course. It wouldn't surprise me if BJ fell in love with Serafina.

And all I have is a stupid little sister and a god-

---

swanky – angeberisch; big deal – tolle Sache; door handle – Türklinke; referee – Schiedsrichter; to burp – rülpsen

mother who gives me pyjamas with pandas on them.

What a miserable weekend.

Monday, 20th April

The battle has begun. Serafina is now my deadly enemy. The rotten, **scheming** little bitch.

During break she **boasted** that she was going to the Cinemaxx today with her brother, BJ and the other boys. If any of the girls wanted to join them, they would have to give her some money.

The stupid chickens immediately chorused: "I'll pay for your ticket", "I'll buy you some popcorn", "I'll **stand you** a Coke" and so on. Serafina nodded graciously in the self-important and **patronising** way that she has.

Then she asked me: "And what about you, Josefine?"

When she says Josefine, I feel like throwing up.

Anyway, all I said was: "Why should I give you money, Princess? I can go to the cinema whenever I want."

---

scheming – intrigant; to boast – angeben; to stand sb sth – jmd. etwas spendieren; patronising – gönnerhaft

She said nothing, and that should have been a warning to me. But naïve as I am, it didn't **register**.

After school, she came up to me again and said, in her sugary-sweet way: "Oh, Jojo Baby," (Jojo Baby – she's absolutely **loopy**) "we've had **second thoughts**. We're not going to the Cinemaxx, we're going to the Multiplex. If you get there before us, go in and save some seats for us."

I still didn't register anything, of course, so I simply said "OK" and trotted off home.

That afternoon I sat in the Multiplex **vigorously** defending an entire row of empty seats, and nobody came.

I was really **pissed off**.

Then, on my way home, I passed the ice-cream parlour and saw the whole lot of them sitting there peacefully enjoying their ices.

I couldn't believe my eyes. That's one more of Serafina's dirty tricks, I thought, suddenly realizing why she had been so sugary-sweet at school. What a **simpleton** I am! I really ought to know that you can't trust Serafina when she's being nice.

Just you wait, I thought to myself. I'll tell you just what I think of you!

---

to register – mitbekommen; loopy – plemplem;
to have second thoughts – sich etwas anders überlegen;
vigorously – energisch; to be pissed off – stinksauer sein;
simpleton – Schwachkopf

So I went in and asked Serafina straight out why she hadn't been at the Multiplex.

To which she, with charmingly **pouting lips**, replied: "Oh, Jojo, you silly old thing! You probably mixed up the names of the cinemas. We agreed to go to the Cinemaxx."

"That's not true," I said.

And before I could really start shouting at her, she said in her sugary-sweet way: "Never mind. Children are always a bit excited when they're allowed to go to the cinema for the first time, and they mix things up. Next time I'll write the name out for you. In block capitals."

They all laughed. Even BJ. Only Justus didn't. I thought that was really nice of him. I felt so terrible. I felt too terrible even to **wreak revenge**.

All I could do was walk out. What an embarrassment! I won't be able to show my face at school ever again.

And at home my mother grumbles because I've been out all day and forgotten to take Flippi along to her **recorder** lesson. A complete waste of time and money. That little toad is about as musical as a **frying pan**.

My mother has already had to buy her two new recorders because Flippi uses her instrument as a

---

pouting lips – gespitzte Lippen; to wreak revenge – auf Rache sinnen; recorder – Blockflöte; frying pan – Bratpfanne

straw to drink her cocoa through. She thinks that's real artistry. Anyone can play a tune on the recorder. She wants to go on TV with her recorder-straw act.

And what does my mother do? She smiles and looks at me as if to say 'isn't the little one sweet?'

The little one's got a screw loose, and things don't get better as she gets older. On the contrary. If my mother doesn't **put her foot down** soon, Flippi will **take over**, and my mother and I will have to ask her permission to go into town for an ice-cream. And I can guarantee that Flippi will stop our pocket money if we refuse to clean her slug cage. Then my mother and I will definitely have to go to bed at eight, and Flippi will sit in the living room until eleven, watching TV and drinking liqueurs.

My mother has no idea of what's **in store for her** if she doesn't put her foot down energetically. She always has endless patience with that child.

And none with me.

---

to put one's foot down – sich durchsetzen; to take over – die Macht übernehmen; to be in store for sb – auf jmd. zukommen

Tuesday, 21st April

My mother is still grumbling.

Mothers know nothing about love.

I had to go to the cinema to see BJ. Or rather for him to see me. Because I've now got a pink strand of hair which looks really cool.

And I now have a new plan. I want to sing in BJ's band. He'll fall in love with me because he certainly knows this is what usually happens. And when I'm BJ's girlfriend, everyone at school will think I'm super cool and will all want to be friends with me. Serafina will be ever so sorry that she didn't let me join her club. But by then it will be too late. When she comes running, begging me to become a member, I'll just smile a frosty smile and say: "**I'm not into** kids' stuff like that. And keep away from me. You're not cool enough."

My mother didn't understand, of course. I tried to explain to her what the most important thing in life is: to look cool and to get the most fantastic boy at school to **chase after** you. And to get kissed at last.

And I told her that my life was terrible, that nobody understood me and that I haven't even got one single pimple yet.

---

to be into sth – an etwas interessiert sein; to chase after – hinterherrennen

She put her arm round me and **stroked** my head to **comfort** me. "Oh darling, I'm so sorry. It's all my fault. I'll look after you better in future, I promise."

Deeply moved, she dropped onto my bed, dramatically took my hands in hers, and looked deep into my eyes. "Jojo, my child, you know that you can talk to me about anything ..."

I know what I had to do: I had to calm her down, otherwise she would spend the whole of next week at my side, planning mother-and-daughter activities.

I patted her on the shoulder to calm her down and said: "Of course I know that, Mummy. I'm fine. I've got everything under control."

My mother: "So what were you doing in the park? On Saturday morning? In your pyjamas??!!"

At the word 'pyjamas', her voice began to **quaver** hysterically. Poor mother!

Obviously my stupid maths teacher has nothing better to do than worry **female single parents**. I was in trouble now. What should I say?

I said what I always say at moments like this: "I lost a **bet**."

This time she wasn't satisfied with my explanation. "You would talk to me about your problems if you had any, wouldn't you, Jojo?"

---

to stroke – streicheln; to comfort – trösten; to quaver – beben; female single parent – allein erziehende Mutter; bet – Wette

"Of course," I said, crossing my index and middle fingers behind my back. This means that what you say will not count as a lie.

My mother embraced me in slight desperation, got up and left the room.

But I still heard her say quietly to herself: "It's all her father's fault."

Which is not far from the truth, for I got the panda pyjamas from his sister. And it was he who insisted on her being my godmother.

Then he ran off, leaving me with the baby panda pyjamas from his sister, while my mother is looking desperately for psychological reasons to explain what I'm doing in the park in my pyjamas.

Yet if I'd told her that I had just managed to avoid going to jail, she would have flipped her lid. Mothers have to be **treated with care** and a lot of understanding.

Thursday, 23rd April

Tonight is the night of all nights.

I've prepared everything. I've laid seven different flowers under my pillow. Because if you put seven different flowers under your pillow, you will defi-

---

to treat with care – schonend behandeln

nitely dream of the man you will marry later. Linda told me so. And I already know who I'll dream about: BJ.

We'll certainly get married in Las Vegas. Because BJ thinks that America is so fabulous.

Friday, 24th April

That was the biggest disappointment of my life.

I dreamed of Benjamin Blümchen!

That just can't be true!

"Will you, Benjamin Blümchen, take this woman Josefine Sonntag to be your **lawful wedded** wife?"

"Taraah!"

I could burst into tears. Our children will either have huge ears or a trunk. Possibly both. People will **peep** into the **pram** and then stare at me in sympathy. Now I know what Dumbo's mother felt like.

And my bed linen is in a **state**. I'm sure to get into trouble. The **dandelion** left disgusting stains, and I should have knocked the earth off the roots of the **daisies** first. The rose wasn't a good idea,

---

lawful wedded – rechtmäßig angetraut; to peep – einen Blick werfen; pram – Kinderwagen; state – Zustand; dandelion – Löwenzahn; daisies – Gänseblümchen

either. One of its thorns has torn a hole in the sheet.

And all that for Benjamin Blümchen! I'm **going nuts**!

Sunday, 26th April

My mother has found the flowers under my pillow, but I had a good explanation. I told her it was a macroidiotic **remedy**, for pimples.

She shrugged her shoulders: "First of all, the word is macrobiotic and secondly you don't have any pimples."

"You see," I said. "It works!"

Before she could take the matter any further, there was a huge **bang** from the living room and my mother rushed out of my bedroom. Flippi had tried out a little chemistry experiment and **blown up** our aquarium.

I'm certain she was trying to make a hydrogen bomb, but nobody believes me anyway. I don't care, because this time she saved me. By the time my mother had finished collecting all the fish, she had

---

to go nuts – wahnsinnig werden; remedy – Heilmittel; bang – Knall; to blow up – in die Luft sprengen

forgotten all about the torn sheet and the pillow. In any case, the damage I caused was nothing compared to an exploding aquarium.

Sometimes having a little sister isn't so bad after all.

I did, however, have to take part in the fish **hunt**, because Flippi said there were still two missing.

When I asked whether we were going to have **fish fingers** for supper, neither of them thought it was funny.

Monday, 27th April

Today was a really cool day.

I saved a fish and rescued an old lady.

It was like this with the fish: I found the two that escaped yesterday. One was in the flower vase – how clever of him. He had a real chance of survival there. Although, my mother always puts super **fertilizer** for cut flowers in the vase so that the fish I saved may suffer from post-fertilizer syndrome later on. We might even produce the first goldfish whale before long. And when he has outgrown the bathtub we'll have to move. To a house with a swimming pool. Not a bad idea.

---

hunt – Jagd; fish fingers – Fischstäbchen; fertilizer – Dünger

The other fish was out of luck. Unfortunately, he had fallen into mother's coffee cup. It was too late to save him. Although it was decaffeinated coffee. But he might have banged his head on the sugar cube and suffered a **fractured skull**. And the doctor fish (oh yes, there is such a thing) was not in his **surgery**. No, he was unable to help the patient. The doctor had been **evacuated**. He's swimming around in a jam jar until my mother has bought a new aquarium. It's also possible that he's forgotten to switch his beeper on.

And now to my second good deed.

I went into town to buy a replacement for the dead fish.

There was a lot of activity outside a telephone box.

An old lady had accidentally shut herself into the telephone box and couldn't get out.

A couple of brainless fourth-graders were **laughing like drains** in front of the door. When the old lady had almost managed to free herself, or should I say finally understood how the mechanism worked, one of the **cheeky lads** stuck his foot in front of the door to stop her from getting out. I twisted his ear for him and opened the door. I did

---

fractured skull – Schädelbruch; surgery – Praxis; evacuated – ausquartiert; to laugh like a drain – sich ausschütten vor Lachen; cheeky lad – frecher Kerl

all this quite unselfishly, **without** any **regard for** my own safety.

The fourth-graders immediately struck up a chorus of: "**Teacher's pet**, teacher's pet!" I got a shock at first, thinking how embarrassing it would be if I had indeed rescued a teacher! Teachers are, of course, the enemies of teenagers, and it's completely uncool to be nice to a teacher. But luckily she turned out not to be a teacher.

The woman was so happy and full of **praise** for me. She offered to reward me with an ice-cream.

Unfortunately, the nearest **ice-cream parlour** was the one where Serafina's club always meets. I felt rather uncomfortable.

I mean rescuing an old lady from a telephone box is one thing, but accepting an invitation to eat ice-cream with her, in public, where BJ might see me – I'm not so sure. She also had a rather strange appearance: she was wearing a hat. A very unusual hat. Strictly speaking, it wasn't really a hat at all, more like an **upside-down** giant **tulip**. It would have looked good in a horror film: 'The Attack of the Killer Tulips'. On her arm she was carrying an old-fashioned doctor's bag. She calls that a handbag! And the curious thing is: she talks to her handbag.

---

without regard for – ohne Rücksicht auf;
teacher's pet – Streber; praise – überschwängliches Lob;
ice-cream parlour – Eisdiele; upside-down –
verkehrt herum; tulip – Tulpe

Calls it Mathilde and asks it for advice on every possible subject. Really loopy!

Unfortunately I couldn't think of any excuse **at short notice**, so I went into the ice-cream parlour with her.

Serafina was there, of course. She and the chickens immediately began cackling "Jojo's got a new friend" and other nasty things. It was really rotten of them!

But the lady bought me a Giant **Sundae**. She ordered two for herself and ate them in double quick time, too!

She was quite charming. But I couldn't get over my embarrassment. I can't remember what she talked about. I couldn't register a thing.

At last I heard her say: "Off you go, then, my child. You will be lucky today."

Strange, isn't it?! I kept looking round all the way home but I couldn't see BJ anywhere. Never mind.

I had completely forgotten about the replacement fish.

---

at short notice – auf die Schnelle; Sundae – Eisbecher

Tuesday, 28th April

Today was, actually, a super day. BJ spoke to me.

In the school library. Our form was there, and so was BJ's.

There was an atlas on the table, and BJ said to me: "Can you pass me the atlas?"

I was so happy that I was **paralysed** with joy, so to speak. I couldn't move a finger.

BJ rolled his eyes and fetched the atlas himself, calling me **'lazybones'**.

Isn't that heavenly! He spoke to me! Twice! I think everything is working out now. BJ and I will soon be together.

I was, however, the victim of yet another embarrassing experience. In the library! Witnessed by BJ!

The librarian suddenly held up a little bear and asked who had lost it.

It was my bear. I was just about to raise my hand and shout 'It's mine' when some clown told her to ask around the first-graders and not to bother seventh- and ninth-graders with kids' stuff. I lowered my hand quickly and began to think desperately how I could get my bear back without **admitting** that it was mine.

---

paralysed – gelähmt; lazybones – Trantüte;
to admit – zugeben

But before I could think up a plan, a loud voice announced. “Jojo. It belongs to Josefine Sonntag. She still plays with **soft toys**.”

That was Serafina, of course. She had seen the bear this morning, when I had taken it out of my jacket pocket and put it in my school bag.

Stupid Serafina had naturally **made fun of me** straight away, saying things like “At last Jojo Baby has found a suitable playmate” and “What a pretty couple” and so on.

A second later she stumbled and **fell full length**.

Serves her right.

The librarian smiled at me encouragingly as she handed me back my little bear, saying: “That really is a sweet bear.”

That was a shock-compliment.

The bear is quite new. New for me, I should say, because he’s really quite old. I’ve had him since yesterday. He’s a kind of **orphan** bear. I’ve adopted him.

I found him on my way home from the ice-cream parlour where I had had an ice-cream with the funny old lady. In a **litter bin** in the middle of town. I really only wanted to throw a chewing-gum wrapper into the bin. When I lifted the lid, I saw a little

---

soft toy – Kuscheltier; to make fun of sb – sich über jmd. lustig machen; to fall full length – der Länge nach hinfallen; orphan – Waise; litter bin – Mülltonne

bear inside. He looked very old fashioned. But if you look him in the eye, he looks very much alive, as if he were just about to say something to you. Very strange.

I felt sorry for the bear. He's tiny, he just about fits inside your hand, so he's really a baby bear. And so alone. I rescued the bear from the rubbish and put him in my pocket. Nothing wrong with that, because someone didn't want him any more.

And when you think of it, he **hadn't been** properly **disposed of**. He was in the section reserved for paper. I'm not even sure how you would dispose of a bear – yellow sack? Compost bin? Nonsense! A bear shouldn't be thrown away at all.

When I got home I bathed him and dried him with the hair dryer, and I let him sleep in my bed with me.

And today I took him to school with me, and stupid Serafina **wound me up** and embarrassed me down to the hair roots because of my bear.

I hate Serafina.

My mother again. She wants me to switch off the light and get to sleep. She says I need more sleep. Any more sleep and my life will be over!

---

to be disposed of – entsorgt werden; to wind sb up – jmd. aufziehen

Wednesday, 29th April

From now on, the bear is my lucky bear. Whenever I have him with me, everything seems to **work out** somehow. It really does!

During the first break I had left my bear in my school bag and didn't see BJ once in the **playground**. During the next break I had the bear in my jeans pocket and BJ passed me no less than three times!

On my way home I was holding the bear in my hand and found a one-Euro piece on the **pavement**.

When I arrived home, my hectic mother ran up to me, gave me a ten-Euro note and said she had to go to the theatre urgently. She told me to buy a pizza for Flippi and me because she hadn't had time to cook anything. That's what I call real luck.

And **it's about time** that my life started working out, too!

---

to work out – gut klappen; playground – Schulhof; pavement – Gehweg; it's about time – es ist an der Zeit

Thursday, 30th April

My mother is worried about me again.

I told her about the bear, that the rubbish-bin bear is a lucky bear that fulfils all my wishes.

But she only gave a mild smile, sighed deeply and pressed me against her angora pullover. I hate that. I always get **fluff** in my eyes and up my nose. That **itches** and makes me sneeze. My eyes water as well. When I had sneezed into her pullover twice and made wet tracks in it with my tears, she finally let me go, saying: "But of course, darling, if you say so. You always had such a gift for imagining things."

What's that supposed to mean? Doesn't she believe me? I look at her angrily and she quickly **adds**: "I believe you, darling, really I do!"

Bah! She doesn't believe a word. She thinks I'm completely dotty, she thinks I'm just **making** things **up** because I don't have a father. She's never short of psycho-explanations like that to quote at me.

---

fluff – Fusseln; to itch – jucken; to add – hinzufügen; to make sth up – etwas erfinden

Monday, 4th May

The bear is really fantastic.

I had forgotten to write my essay. For German. I secretly **kept a firm grip** on my bear and kept thinking 'She won't ask me to read, she won't ask me to read' and Mrs Bertram really didn't ask me to read my essay. Fantastic, isn't it?

And during break I wished that Linda and Serafina would have an argument. And it worked! The bear is fantastic. Serafina had borrowed Linda's new **hair slide** and broken it. Normally, Serafina would then say something like: "Don't **take on** so! I went to a super party wearing your hair slide yesterday. What a wonderful end for a hair slide!" and Linda would say nothing.

But today Linda cried, and Serafina got annoyed and said she didn't want anything to do with **cry-babies**.

Then Linda came over to me and I **consoled** her. Now she's my best friend again.

Nothing new as far as BJ is concerned. But I suddenly **realized** with shock that he doesn't even have my telephone number. Suppose he wants to ring

---

to keep a firm grip – fest drücken; hair slide – Haarspange; to take on – sich anstellen; cry-baby – Heulsuse; to console sb – jmd. trösten; to realize – sich bewusst werden

me and make a date? Linda says that doesn't matter. He doesn't even know my name.

Justus said hello to me in the playground today. I thought it was very nice of him. Perhaps he can give BJ my telephone number. And tell him my name.

Tuesday, 5th May

My mother is still angry with Flippi because of the bomb in the aquarium. She has told Flippi that she has to pay for the damage out of her pocket money. My mother was very proud of this tough **child-rearing measure** of hers.

Then she increased Flippi's pocket money so that she can finish paying the **instalments** by the time she goes to university.

That can't be true! What am I expected to learn from that? My mother should think about things like that. That will have negative educational consequences at a later stage. What do members of the Sonntag family have to do to get more pocket money? Blow up an aquarium.

---

child-rearing measure – Erziehungsmaßnahme;
instalment – Rate

Wednesday, 6th May

I was in town again today to meet Linda because she wanted to tell me a secret about Serafina.

It wasn't a very interesting secret because I already knew about the colour of her hair. I know that Serafina has mousey-brown hair that she regularly dyes.

Then Linda told me her own secret. She is not **actually** in love with BJ but with Patrick and is slightly in love with Justus. Then I told Linda that Justus had said hello to me, and she said she thought that was really **rotten** of me. I can't do anything about that, can I? She's been friendly with Serafina too long. She's already just as **bitchy**.

That put us both in a bad mood, and Linda said she had to go home and bone up her maths for the next class test. That was, God knows, the worst excuse Linda has ever thought up.

I wandered around town a bit longer, keeping an eye open for the strange old lady who had treated me to an ice-cream.

I thought she might like to have someone to chat with again.

But I didn't see her anywhere. Then I went home and – would you believe it – started boning up my maths!

---

actually – wirklich; rotten – gemein; bitchy – gemein

Thursday, 7th May

Today I met the old lady again.

She was sitting on a bench in the park. She **beckoned** me across to her and asked me if I'd like an ice-cream. I panicked at the thought of the ice-cream parlour and said: "No, thank you."

"Not in the ice-cream parlour," she said. "Here."

Chatting cheerfully to her handbag she pulled an ice-cream sundae and a spoon out of it, smiled, and handed them both to me.

I sat down on the bench beside her and started eating my ice-cream. She pulled another sundae for herself out of the handbag, then another. She always eats two sundaes, she says, **for reasons of balance**.

I don't know exactly what she meant, but it sounded **convincing**. So I wanted another one, too, for reasons of balance. But she said too much sugar was not good for girls of my age. They gave you pimples.

Hey! What a super tip. On my way home I bought myself a kilo of sugar. Let's see whether I can get into puberty yet or not.

At any rate, the old lady talked and talked. She has a way of asking questions and then immedi-

---

to beckon – winken; for reasons of balance – dem Gleichgewicht zuliebe; convincing – überzeugend; at any rate – jedenfalls

ately answering them herself, so you don't actually have to say much. She carries out the entire conversation. Her own part, of course, but she also takes over my part. That goes **rather** like this: "Do you enjoy going to school? – But of course you like going to school. Everything has got much nicer in he meantime. It's simply more fun for today's kids. Teachers aren't as strict as they used to be. – Or do you still have any of the really old-fashioned '**hands-on' teachers**? – No, I'm sure you don't. Nowadays they're all young, modern people, too." She doesn't really need me, but it's better to have me sitting beside her. Then the other people won't think she's a bit strange – talking to herself like that.

And because she doesn't really need me for conversation, my thoughts sometimes wander off, so that when she really expects a reply from me, I don't know what the question was.

Then comes the embarrassing part. Then she brings her handbag into the conversation. "Mathilde," she says. "Mathilde, I don't think our young friend is listening **particularly** attentively."

The old lady is certainly very strange, but **nice with it**. Her name is Klarafina. And she wants me to use her first name. That's cool for someone of her age.

---

rather – ungefähr; hands-on teachers – autoritäre Pauker; particularly – besonders; nice with it – auf eine nette Art

Today she suddenly asked me whether I was satisfied with the way my life was working out. I waited for her to answer her question for me, but she stopped talking and looked at me questioningly. So she wanted me to answer this question myself. I thought for a moment, then told her that everything was working out wonderfully, especially now that I have my bear.

She leaned back **contentedly** and said that that was wonderful. He would do his work.

No idea what she really meant by that.

When I asked her, she smiled and **winked** at me. She said she was happy that I had found him at last, and that it was a good thing for a girl of my age to have a **protector**.

Exactly, a 'protector'. Everyone would certainly run away if I pulled my bear out of my pocket and said: 'Disappear, or my bear will spit at you!' But I said nothing.

Then I told her that a couple of strange things had happened since I found the bear.

"That was only to be expected," she said.

That's what I call a cool reaction. Not like my mother, who always thinks she's **failed** to bring me up properly.

Basically, I agree with her, of course.

---

contentedly – zufrieden; to wink – zuzwinkern; protector – Beschützer; to fail – versagen

When you think that I'm sitting here on a park bench with an old lady who talks to a handbag which she keeps ice-cream sundaes in. I'm not sure whether this is the right company for a thirteen-year-old.

Where are all the fantastic friends I'm supposed to have? When do I get to go to a disco? And who keeps ringing me up asking if he can take me out??! Well?

Forget it. My mother has certainly done her best. Even mothers are not perfect.

Klarafina wanted to know more about my bear, saying that he was a very special bear. She was absolutely excited, which I found a bit **exaggerated**. At her age you should be a bit calmer and not flip your lid about a little bear, attributing him with all kinds of secrets. He brought me luck. That's all there is to it.

But Klarafina was of the opinion that the bear would change my life. Now all my wishes would be fulfilled.

So much the better.

So please, dear bear, make BJ ring me up and say that he wants a date with me. Thank you.

---

exaggerated – übertrieben

Sunday, 10th May

I can't believe it: he rang up!

Or **rather** Justus rang me up. At first I thought he would pass the phone to BJ right away because BJ is perhaps too shy to ring me up himself. But no. Justus asked me if I'd like to go to a basketball match with him.

Then I realized: BJ asked Justus to invite me so that he can **turn up** later and meet me as if **by chance**. So I agreed immediately, of course. But I didn't say anything to **betray** the fact that I had seen through their little game!

Maybe that's something to do with the bear. That's all right by me.

I looked completely cool: red **patent-leather boots**, a red-and-white miniskirt, a tiny, tummy-free blue top with white stars. Perfect – I looked like a walking American flag. So BJ will see that we're both on the same wavelength: America fans.

When Justus came to pick me up, he gave me a rather surprised look and said we were going to a basketball match, not to a disco.

I told him this was my basketball outfit. I always wore it when I went to watch a match. He asked me to name him a couple of basketball teams and I

---

rather – vielmehr; to turn up – aufkreuzen; by chance – zufällig; to betray – verraten; patent-leather boots – Lackstiefel replied that I couldn't think of the names at the moment but never missed a match.

Justus grinned and said he could tell I was a real professional. Then he said he thought he should mention that we would be sitting in the **stand** and that there were no **vacancies** in the cheerleader team in case I was hoping to join them …

I smiled at him and said: "Keep cool! I know what I'm doing."

He raised his eyebrows and asked me whether I didn't want to at least tie a scarf round my bare tummy. I would **catch cold** otherwise.

What an idea! I spent an hour sticking a tattoo of the American flag beside my **belly button** in order to show BJ that **I'm keen on** the USA, too. I was certainly not going to tie a scarf round it now!

The match was great. Justus's favourite team won, we drank Cokes and ate hot dogs, and four people wanted to be photographed with me, asking me which cheerleader group I belonged to.

It was really quite good. Except that BJ didn't come. I didn't want to ask Justus where BJ was because he might have been disappointed that I had seen through their little plan.

None of Justus's other friends were there, either. We were the only ones. Not the only ones at the

---

stand – Tribüne; vacancies – freie Plätze; to catch cold – sich erkälten; belly button – Bauchnabel; to be keen on sth – auf etwas stehen

match, of course. But the only ones from our school.

It's really a pity. The first time I go out with a boy, there's no one there to see me.

But I'm worried about BJ. I hope nothing's happened to him.

Monday, 11th May

BJ is alive, everything is OK.

He must be getting a little forgetful. He had a gig yesterday. A school dance at the Luisenschule. Everyone was there.

Linda told me she had gone there with Serafina and the chickens. They've **made up their quarrel**, by the way. Linda bought herself a new hair slide, gave it to Serafina and apologized for **turning on the waterworks** because of her old one. Serafina accepted both her apology and the hair slide, and Linda was allowed to go to the school dance.

Serafina thinks that there are better boys at the Luisenschule than at our school. Linda told me that unfortunately the girls all looked better than us, too. She almost got into another **argument** with

---

to make up a quarrel – einen Streit beilegen; to turn on the waterworks – auf die Tränendrüsen drücken; argument – Auseinandersetzung

Serafina for saying that. But Linda quickly added: "All except you, Serafina." And Serafina was satisfied.

But I'm rather disappointed at BJ all the same. How could he forget such an important date?

In order to give BJ a second chance, I told Justus we could go to another basketball match again soon. Justus thought that was a good idea.

Wednesday, 13th May

I think my bear has **screwed** things **up**.

I went to a basketball game with Justus again and BJ didn't turn up.

I have to talk to Klarafina urgently. But how can we meet? I don't have her telephone number, her address, anything. I only know her first name. That's not really enough information to contact someone. I can't really go to the police and say: "I'm looking for a lady who talks to her handbag, eats tons of ice-cream sundaes, is called Klarafina and talks nonsense about magic bears."

Klarafina – where are you???

---

to screw sth up – etwas verpatzen

Thursday, 14th May

Something sensational has happened: I was in the public library, and who did I meet? No, not BJ, but Klarafina. That in itself isn't the sensation, of course. It's what Klarafina told me. But one thing after the other:

Klarafina was sitting at a table and eating an ice-cream sundae. In the middle of the library. She's got a nerve! There were already two empty sundae glasses on the table beside her.

I went up to her and sat down beside her.

She asked me slightly reproachfully why I hadn't arrived **punctually** and told me that she had already eaten my ice-cream.

We hadn't agreed to meet at a certain time, but I didn't want to tell her that **straight out**. It might have upset her.

Instead I asked her how she was **preserving** the balance.

"Three is actually a magic number. At least for us witches," was her reply.

"For us witches?"

"Yes. And you are one of us now, Jojo."

I looked at her with wide eyes and asked her what she meant.

---

punctually – pünktlich; straight out – geradeheraus; to preserve – bewahren

"But Jojo, didn't you tell me that your bear can do strange things for you?"

She was right, of course. He could.

"He's a magic bear. And he doesn't perform his magic for just anyone. He is meant for a witch," she said quite calmly as she ate the rest of the ice-cream.

She's **gone** completely **crackers**. I don't believe a word she says.

It's the ice-cream. Klarafina is suffering from sugar shock and talking nonsense.

I said goodbye and hurried home.

Wow! If I tell my poor mother, she'll **reproach** herself for having brought me up all wrong and **deprive** herself voluntarily **of the right** to look after me!

Friday morning, 15th May

A witch!

What nonsense! Am I **Snow White**, or is my name Gretel? I ask you! Even as a child I never believed in

---

to go crackers – überschnappen; to reproach – Vorwürfe machen; to deprive of a right – ein Recht entziehen; Snow White – Schneewittchen

Father Christmas, so it's a bit late now for someone to start telling me about witches.

But theoretically, just assuming that there might be some **grain of truth** in it. Supposing I were a witch and the bear was a magic bear. So what? I mean, what does that mean for me? Must I move into some **dilapidated** old **gingerbread** house in the forest? Will I grow a **wart** on my nose now? Will I exchange my bike for a broom? How exactly does a modern witch live? Does she regularly have her warts removed cosmetically? Does she ride around on a **turbocharged vacuum cleaner**?

It's all too silly for words.

So I'll just have to talk to Klarafina about it.

Friday evening, 15th May

Klarafina was nowhere to be found.

Not even in the public library.

But seeing as I was there anyway, I borrowed a **pile** of books on witches. You'll find them in the 'Women's Literature' section, by the way. It was a

---

grain of truth – Körnchen Wahrheit; dilapidated – heruntergekommen; gingerbread – Lebkuchen; wart – Warze; turbocharged – mit Turboantrieb; vacuum cleaner – Staubsauger; pile – Stapel

big, heavy stack of books, and at first I wanted to make the pile **float** along beside me. As a test, so to speak. But then I thought better of it. I don't have to show everyone that I'm a witch. At least not before I'm absolutely sure of it myself. So I simply carried the books home like any other normal person.

So here I sit with the books on the table and have to decide which to read first: 'Caught in one's own **spell'**, 'When the broom refuses to rise', 'The **lighter side of** witchcraft', 'Witches' **curses**: once spoken – never broken' or 'The little ABC for young witches in puberty'.

My mother was just here, saw the books, felt my forehead and murmured something about taking me to the doctor's.

I tried to calm her down. I told her everything was OK, she needn't worry. There was a possibility that I might be a witch. I had this information from a **reliable source**. If she had a **wish** she wanted **granted**, or if I could magic anything for her, she need only say the word.

She was completely **gobsmacked**, and I had to promise her faithfully not to say anything about this

---

to float – schweben; spell – Bann; the lighter side of sth – etwas leicht gemacht; curse – Fluch; reliable source – zuverlässige Quelle; to grant a wish – einen Wunsch erfüllen; to be gobsmacked – von den Socken sein

to anyone. She's going to look for a specialist. I can tell him or her all about it.

My mother is so out of touch with reality.

Sunday, 17th May

Thank you, Klarafina! She tells me that I now belong to the **sorority** of witches, then disappears into thin air! I haven't seen her for days. The earth must have swallowed her up.

In the meantime I've decided to approach the entire witch business **from the scientific angle** – I'm going to carry out a series of experiments. Either I can cast spells or I can't.

First I tried to make Flippi grow rabbit's ears. But I don't know whether the spell worked. Flippi refused to show me her ears. She simply screamed at me to get out of her room, put her hands over both ears and **yelled** that her ears were none of my business. I must be absolutely **bonkers**, she said.

It was only about an hour later that I had the chance to pull her hair back and inspect her ears. But her ears looked quite normal again. A little more pointed, perhaps, and maybe a little more

---

sorority – Schwesternschaft; from the scientific angle – vom wissenschaftlichen Standpunkt aus; to yell – schreien; to be bonkers – übergeschnappt sein

furry than usual, but I couldn't get a proper look at them because Flippi **punched** me right in the eye. Perhaps spells cast by beginner witches don't last very long.

Then I went back to my room and continued practising. I tried to get the **hands of my clock** to move backwards. But to be honest I was not very successful.

Then I remembered my bear. Perhaps I have to hold the bear in my hand when I'm doing magic, so I picked up the bear and concentrated as hard as I could on getting the hands of the clock to move forwards. That worked wonderfully well.

OK. Then I told the bear I wanted my mother to come into my room now and tell me she is going to increase my pocket money.

And my mother did in fact come into my room, if only to tell me that I should finally start doing my homework.

Well, at least half the spell worked.

I think I need a bit more practice. I'll soon work out. Perhaps the bear has to get used to me first.

I'll take him to school tomorrow. My first **victim** will be Serafina.

---

furry – pelzig; to punch – boxen; hands of the clock – Uhrzeiger; victim – Opfer

Monday, 18th May

My first day as a witch is a great success.

With the bear in my pocket, I first told Serafina what I really thought about her. If she gets **cheeky**, I thought, I'll turn her into a wild pig.

I told her she was the worst friend anyone could have. That she was egoistic and rotten, and that girls who had her as a friend didn't need enemies. And that she shouldn't go on pretending to be something better. She might perhaps be a little prettier than most and might wear better clothes, but that was nothing **to get conceited about**. Apart from which she was pretty stupid at school. She should spend more time learning rather than constantly dyeing her hair.

Then I held my breath for a second to wait and see if she tried to hit me. But nothing happened.

She didn't say a word. She just stared at me, and I saw a suspicious **glint** in her eyes. Then she walked off.

Then I went up to Linda and told her that I was founding a club of my own. The Club of the Unkissed. Every member pays two Euros into the **kitty**, and the first girl to kiss a boy gets **the lot**.

---

cheeky – frech; to get conceited about sth – sich etwas einbilden auf; glint – Glitzern; kitty – gemeinsame Kasse; the lot – das Ganze

The good thing about my club is that every member can be in love with whom she likes. And those who don't want to be in love needn't be. But they have to pay the two Euros all the same.

Linda thought she would have to discuss it with Serafina first to see whether it would annoy her.

Oh, Linda has still got so much to learn!

I got the idea of a club of my own from my mother. Yesterday evening she came back into my room after the witch episode and wanted to have one of her 'I'm-your-friend-you-can-tell-me-everything' talks with me. I wanted to calm her down, so I graciously **condescended**.

She definitely wanted to solve a problem for me, but I couldn't think of a suitable one for her to solve. Then I told her about Serafina and her club, and that Serafina doesn't want me in it and is always so rotten.

My mother's **enthusiasm** began to flow.

She loves it when I have problems. She swings into action and produces a load of 'very simple' solutions. I think all this activity gives her the feeling of being a real mother.

So she **suggested** to me that I should simply found a club of my own and exclude Serafina. Then she would see what it feels like.

---

to condescend – sich herablassen;
enthusiasm – Begeisterung; to suggest – vorschlagen

Not a bad idea when you think it came from a mother. Maybe there's hope for her yet.

When she asked me whether that had **sorted out** the witch thing, I had a feeling that it would be a good idea to say yes. She **gathered up** all my witch books and said she would take them back to the library. I hadn't read any of them, but I didn't want to **arouse her suspicions**, so I pretended everything was OK. If I want to, I can magic the books back at any time, of course.

She was very **relieved**, and trotted off to Flippi's room. She was probably on a round of motherly talks, and would be checking Flippi for possible abnormalities.

But she's out of luck with Flippi, who can wind her round her little finger.

If Flippi does something wrong, our mother generally only finds it **'delightful'**, in contradiction to all theories of child-rearing.

Like the time Flippi sold her maths textbook at the **jumble sale**.

Flippi desperately wanted to have a stall at the jumble sale and pestered my mother until at last she said yes.

---

to sort out – in Ordnung bringen; to gather up – einsammeln; to arouse suspicions – Verdacht erregen; relieved – erleichtert; delightful – entzückend; jumble sale – Flohmarkt

But my mother told her: "You may only sell old stuff, nothing valuable."

"Of course," said Flippi.

But that means nothing to her.

To be on the safe side, I kept my bedroom door locked for two days, because Flippi is without scruples.

A couple of days later, Flippi's maths teacher rang my mother up highly indignant protesting about the way my mother treated school property.

During the call it became clear that Flippi had told her teacher she couldn't do her maths homework because my mother had said she should sell her old maths book at the jumble sale because she wouldn't allow Flippi to keep old things in her bedroom.

The teacher was pretty angry and **lectured** my mother on the fact that this book had been school property for generations and that she had no right to **pass judgement on** such a book. It was a valuable one.

My mother kept her cool and said it couldn't be that valuable if Flippi had only got fifty Cents for it. She offered to transfer the **proceeds from the sale** to the school.

---

to lecture sb – jmd. einen Vortrag halten; to pass judgement on sth – etwas beurteilen; proceeds from the sale – Verkaufserlös

Sometimes my mother is really fantastic. She had no idea of what had really happened but was annoyed at the teacher's cheeky approach and **stuck up for** Flippi.

Afterwards she grumbled at Flippi and had to buy her a new maths textbook, too, but she wasn't really annoyed at Flippi.

When I sold my school poetry textbook at a jumble sale, however, (I hate poems) she flipped her lid.

With me, it's a completely different matter. Just because I'm a couple of years older.

And I haven't even reached puberty yet. So I still come under the **Child Protection Act**, don't I?

Tuesday, 19th May

Serafina hates me. She started hating me yesterday. Because I dared to talk to her like that.

That's something at least. Linda told me about it. Secretly, when Serafina wasn't anywhere near us. Because the chickens are no longer allowed to speak to me.

Linda told me that Serafina has also forbidden her brother from speaking to me.

---

to stick up for sb – zu jmd. halten; Child Protection Act – Kinderschutzgesetz

Somehow my club isn't really a best-seller. I'm the only member, and that's pretty boring.

That's what you get for taking your mother's advice! It's all so long ago in her case, and I'm sure she's mixed things up a bit. Everything is different **nowadays** anyway.

I ought to force my mother to become a member of my club and to pay me two Euros. But she isn't unkissed any more.

Well, I suppose the most I could do would be to change the name from the Club of the Unkissed to the Club of Not-Kissed-for-a-Long-Time. Because my mother has certainly not kissed anyone since my father went away, and that's ages ago.

Hang on! I've got it! That's the best idea of the century: I'll found a club to find new husbands for mothers. Because if my mother had another husband, she would certainly leave me in peace. Then she would have problems of her own and not be wanting to solve mine all the time.

I'll put an advertisement in the newspaper.

Maybe Klarafina might like to join, too.

Or should I forget all about the club and **apologize** to Serafina?

---

nowadays – heutzutage; hang on! – Moment mal!;
to apologize – sich entschuldigen

Wednesday, 20th May

Actually I really did want to apologize to Serafina.

I went up to her during break and said: "We've got to talk." I had my hand in my pocket. Suddenly I felt the bear. And at that moment I had second thoughts. A witch has no need to apologize. So I went on: "If you apologize, not only to me but to the others, then I'll talk to you again."

Serafina was so angry that her eyes went as big as **saucers** and her voice turned into a **squeak**. How did I dare say things like that? Who did I think I was? That was no way to talk to her!

Somehow that didn't annoy me at all. I simply smiled and said: "Just think about it, baby." Then I turned round and walked away.

I like being a witch because nobody can harm me.

Thursday, 21st May

Justus has just rung up again and asked whether I'd like to go to the basketball match with him. There you are! He doesn't allow himself **to be intimidated** by his stupid sister.

---

saucer – Untertasse; squeak – Piepsen; to be intimidated – sich einschüchtern lassen

But I told him that I don't want to go to another basketball match.

I never meet BJ there. Somehow the bear doesn't seem to be able **to pull it off**.

In order to make it easier for the bear, I told Justus that I'd like to go to one of the gigs where BJ's band plays.

Justus said that everyone else would be there.

So they would, I said, thinking **primarily** of BJ.

Justus had to think about that for a moment. Then he agreed. He said it would be better if we met inside. And when I asked why, he hummed and grawled before finally agreeing to pick me up from home.

Boys are strange creatures.

So, now the bear can do his job. It shouldn't be too difficult for him to make BJ appear at his own gig.

Incidentally, it could be that I have a Justus allergy. He doesn't seem **to suit me** somehow. Every time he rings up or we meet, I get a strange **tickling** in the tummy and feel a bit **peaky**.

---

to pull sth off – etwas hinkriegen; primarily – in erster Linie; to suit sb – jmd. gut tun, wohl bekommen; tickling – Kribbeln; peaky – flau

Friday, 22nd May

The secret commando project 'A Husband for Mother' has been **launched**.

It wasn't easy. I went down to the newspaper office with Flippi. But they refused to accept an advertisement placed by children. Although Flippi immediately reacted with great **presence of mind**, pointing to me and hissing indignantly that I wasn't a child but a grown-up. She even said I was her mother. When the man looked me up and down and cast a questioning glance at Flippi, she kept her cool and continued: "My mother has **growth problems**. But she's undergoing treatment."

I wanted to demonstrate my motherhood by **rapping** Flippi **over the head with my knuckles** and saying, in a critical, motherly way: "Don't be so cheeky, young lady!"

But Flippi was so angry that she forgot the role she was playing, boxed me on the arm and called me an old **swamp cow**.

I tried to smile and said to the man: "That's what happens if you bring your children up too **liberally**." But it was too late to save the situation. He asked us to leave the office immediately.

---

to launch sth – etwas ins Rollen bringen; presence of mind – Geistesgegenwart; growth problems – Wachstumsstörung; to rap over the head with the knuckles – eine Kopfnuss geben; swamp cow – Sumpfkuh; liberally – freizügig

We didn't give up so quickly, of course. We simply phoned the advertisement in from home. We had to phone twice because they asked me how old I was. Although I had tried to make my voice sound older. Then Flippi rang up, and succeeded **first time round**. Flippi's voice has a certain tone that **brooks** no contradiction.

So the project has been launched. The ad will be published. Flippi and I are as excited as if we were getting married ourselves.

Thursday afternoon, 28th May

A complete **flop**.

Mother's potential marriage partners **called**. We told our mother nothing about it in advance so that she would act quite naturally and not get so excited. I'm sure that you get quite excited when you meet the man you are soon going to marry and you might say something silly. And as most of what my mother says is silly anyway, I thought it would be better to tell her nothing and not make her nervous. But it was all **in vain**. My mother screwed it all up anyway.

---

first time round – beim ersten Mal; to brook – dulden; flop – Reinfall; to call – zu Besuch kommen; in vain – vergebens

Incidentally, I made Flippi pay for half of the ad because it is, of course, in her interest, too, to **provide** our mother with problems of her own again. Flippi agreed immediately. My mother must have got on her nerves quite a lot recently!

So Flippi and I **lay in wait**. To be precise, we were hanging about in the hall, waiting to see what would happen. You never know. Maybe our mother will need support. It's such a long time since she last got married.

The doorbell rang. My mother called to me to see who was there.

That was not the plan. She was to open the front door so that the marriage candidate would see her first and fall in love with her at once.

I said I couldn't go to the door.

She called to Flippi, who **whined** that she couldn't go either.

My mother came storming out of her sewing room **in a paddy** past the two of us. But before she opened the door, she grumbled at us for standing around in the hall doing nothing. We could at least open the door.

Flippi said she had hurt both her hands and held up her **paws** pathetically in the air. Shit, that should

---

to provide – versorgen; to lay in wait – auf der Lauer liegen; to whine – plärren; in a paddy – aufgebracht; paw – Pfote

have been my excuse. And when my mother asked ironically what was preventing me from opening the door, I said my legs were hurting and I couldn't walk. A pretty weak excuse, admittedly, but I couldn't think of a better one.

So she was pretty annoyed by the time she got to the door, with her **tape-measure** still round her neck, a **pincushion** on her wrist and five pins in her mouth. I wanted to open the door for her and tried to persuade her to put some lipstick on, but she just pushed me aside. At any rate, she didn't look very **impressive**.

She opened the front door.

A man with a bunch of flowers was standing outside. A fat, old guy of at least forty, perhaps even sixty. He looked just right – she would certainly have plenty of problems with him, I thought.

The man was rather nervous. He was **perspiring freely**. He **cleared his throat**, made a little **hint of a bow** and held the flowers out to my mother. "Good day, Ferdinand Friedrich is my name. I've come about the advertisement."

My mother looked at Mr Friedrich in a somewhat irritated way, thinking that he was trying to sell her some flowers. She said she didn't need any.

---

tape-measure – Metermaß; pincushion – Nadelkissen; impressive – beeindruckend; to perspire freely – heftig schwitzen; to clear one's throat – sich räuspern; hint of a bow – Andeutung einer Verbeugung

Mr Friedrich smiled but went on holding out the flowers. "I appreciate **modesty** in a woman. That gives us at least one thing in common." Then he took one step forward.

But my mother blocked his path. She really has forgotten how to win over a man!

Mr Friedrich became even more nervous, cleared his throat several more times, and tried again: "I regard myself as a gardener, you see, and …"

My mother suddenly thought she knew what it was all about: "You're at the wrong house. It's Mrs Lüpke who's looking for a gardener."

She was about to shut the door again, but Friedrich wasn't **to be put off** so easily. He pushed the flowers through the narrow slit in the door and murmured: "How nice! You have a sense of humour, too. I'm sure we'll get on very well together."

Suddenly my mother beamed and opened the door again. "Oh, please excuse me. You must be a new driver from the theatre. But I'm **nowhere near** finished. The costumes weren't to be picked up until this evening."

To which Mr Friedrich replied: "If you want to go to the theatre and if that will relieve your bore-

---

modesty – Bescheidenheit; to be put off – sich abwimmeln lassen; nowhere near – noch lange nicht

dom, **I'm quite prepared** to take you. Your advertisement said: 'I'm looking for a man who can relieve my boredom'. I'm exactly the right man for you."

Only now did my mother gradually begin to realize what was happening. But instead of asking him to come in at last, she turned to us and stared at us with that **penetrating** look of hers. Flippi can meet such a look with an expression of innocence. I can't. My mother knew what was going on.

She turned back briefly to Mr Friedrich, told him that it was all, unfortunately, a misunderstanding, and slammed the door in his face. That cost several flowers their heads, for Mr Friedrich was unable to match the withdrawal of his **posy** to the speed with which my mother slammed the door.

Then she turned to us. We quickly tried to slink back to our rooms unnoticed, but it was too late. She stopped us, placed her hands firmly on her hips and **let loose**. She demanded an explanation **on the spot**.

To be honest, I hadn't thought that she would need an explanation. I thought she would see a man, fall in love, the two would marry and Flippi and I would be left in peace. I wasn't at all prepared for the present situation.

---

to be quite prepared – gerne bereit sein;
penetrating – durchdringend; posy – Blumenstrauß;
to let loose – loslegen; on the spot – auf der Stelle

I looked at Flippi. She looked at her fingernails.

Neither of us said a word. This could go on for ever. Our mother's nerves are good. She could keep us standing here for three weeks if neither of us says anything.

I thought for a moment and decided to try the truth. That's not very creative but better than **staying rooted** to the spot. I started off with: "Well ... we thought ... you're always so alone ... and you work so much ... so we ..."

That's as far as I got. "Put an ad in the newspaper?" asked my mother, raising her eyebrows.

Flippi had loosened up a little by now and, still sticking to the truth, unnecessarily corrected her: "A marriage advertisement!"

My mother **gasped for breath** and wanted to shout at us. But Flippi put on her sweetest smile, which she does very well, and I looked so **dejected**, which I do very well.

My mother smiled. She was touched. "But children, that's not the way to do it. There's much more to it than that!"

"What?" asked Flippi.

My mother: "Well, **romance**, for example. That's very important. And ..."

She got no further, for there was another ring at

---

staying rooted – wie angewurzelt dastehen; to gasp for breath – nach Luft schnappen; dejected – zerknirscht; romance – Romantik

the doorbell. She threw us a **threatening** glance – surely not another …? – and opened the door. Mr Baumann, my maths teacher, was standing at the door with a box of chocolates. At first I was paralysed by shock, but suddenly I got the use of my legs back and **beat a hasty retreat**.

Flippi ran up to him, whispering that he should be romantic – our mother loved that!

My mother was very relieved that it was only my maths teacher and not a marriage candidate. She was really **exuberant** friendly and invited him in.

Flippi followed hard on his heels.

My mother offered him something to drink. He looked at Flippi, who nodded encouragingly and silently mouthed the word 'romance'.

Whereupon he began: "Where we drink and where we love: there the world is rich and free!"

My mother looked at him in irritation and put the coffee pot down again, fetched a bottle of apple juice and said: "Perhaps you'd prefer a glass of fruit juice. You've probably already drunk enough coffee today."

Flippi rushed into my room giving the thumbs-up sign and told me what had happened. Everything hunky-dory.

---

threatening – drohend; to beat a hasty retreat – schnell abhauen; exuberant – überschwänglich

I looked at her **in horror** and told her that the man was my maths teacher. So much the better, said Flippi.

"That's fantastic, then you'll finally get good marks for maths if he marries Mummy."

I told her that I already get good marks, that I certainly won't call him Daddy and that I'd hate to have a teacher in the family. That would be worse than terrible. I told her to go straight back into the living room and **prevent** the marriage.

Flippi toddled off, and I'm sitting here biting my nails.

Later on Thursday, 28th May

It was bound to go wrong.

I don't have to call him Daddy. Flippi told me that Baumann had talked a load of nonsense and even recited a poem: "Thou art just like a flower, so lovely, sweet and pure; I look at thee, and longing is with me evermore!"

My mother began to get more and more worried, and when he went down on his knees and **proposed marriage**, my mother began to realize what was

---

in horror – voller Entsetzen; to prevent – verhindern; to propose marriage – einen Heiratsantrag machen going on. She explained that it was all a terribly embarrassing mix-up.

She said she had put an ad in the paper because … because … she wanted to sell her vacuum cleaner. Was Mr Baumann interested?

The mix-up embarrassed him so much that he actually bought the vacuum cleaner.

And my mother is now furious with me because we no longer have a vacuum cleaner.

That's not my fault. She should have thought of something else to sell.

Flippi suggested that mother could perhaps ask Mr Baumann if he wanted to sell her his vacuum cleaner, because he must now have two. And he certainly hadn't wanted to buy hers. He had only bought it **to cover up** the fact that he wanted to marry my mother.

Unless, of course, my mother should decide to marry him. Then she'd get her vacuum cleaner back. Actually, we would then have two vacuum cleaners …

At that point my mother gave a hysterical scream and told us both to go to our rooms immediately and not to come out until we were eighteen.

To make things even worse, Baumann took the chocolates away with him.

I could use them now – as food for my nerves.

---

to cover up sth – etwas vertuschen

And the chocolate might even give me a couple of pimples.

No chocolates, no pimples, no vacuum cleaner, no husband for mother – what a flop!

Friday, 29th May

My mother and I have **made it up**.

That's quite easy to do. You only have to go into her sewing room, sit down beside her for a bit and say how fantastic you think her work is and how you want to do exactly the same thing when you grow up. And if you then tell her how much you love her and that she's the best mother in the world, then everything is OK again.

I had to get **on good terms with** her urgently, because tomorrow is BJ's concert, and I'm going to it, with Justus. I need a mother who's in a good mood.

In order to make sure, I asked her for her advice on what to wear for the concert. Her enthusiasm immediately caught fire. She loves being asked for advice. She spent at least an hour draping various pieces of cloth over my shoulder, making **sketches**

---

to make it up – sich versöhnen; to be on good terms with sb – mit jmd. auf gutem Fuß stehen; sketch – Entwurf

and **ruffling hems** until I told her I didn't want to make a lot of work for her. I said I'd wear something from my **wardrobe**. She wouldn't hear of it, and insisted on sewing something for me.

I have to say one thing: I make great **sacrifices** to put my mother in a peaceable mood again.

I'd better take my rucksack with me tomorrow – the one in which I keep my normal gear. If necessary, I can get changed somewhere on the way. With my mother, you never know when her creativity might run away with her!

Recently, when my class went to the theatre, she designed a rococo mini-dress for me. I've never felt so embarrassed. It looked as if I had forgotten to finish dressing.

When I wanted to leave my coat at the **cloakroom**, an elderly gentleman quickly wrapped his jacket around my legs because he thought I didn't have a skirt on. I tried to convince him that the final **frill** below my belly button was really a skirt, but he was so shocked and had made me so uncertain that I asked for my coat back.

Then I spent two hours sitting in the theatre in my coat.

---

to ruffle – raffen; hem – Bordüre; wardrobe – Kleiderschrank; sacrifice – Opfer; cloakroom – Garderobe; frill – Rüsche

It wasn't easy, either, because the **usherette** told me that the cloakrooms were downstairs and that I should leave my coat there. Then I opened my coat and told her that I had been in such a hurry that I had been a little forgetful. She nodded understandingly and quickly **enfolded** my legs in the coat again.

With my mother's designs, you have to be prepared. You never know …

But she is really convincing. In matters of taste she will not be contradicted. She must have learned that from Flippi.

It's a mystery to me how my mother always gets me to wear her absurd creations.

She might well have sold the **emperor** his new clothes.

Sunday, 31st May

It was so-o-o-o fantastic!

I went to BJ's concert with Justus. BJ is so-o-o sweet! He stared at me all the time he was singing. Then he came up to Justus and me, looked critically at my hair and asked me whether I had had a difference of opinion with our kitchen **whisk**.

---

usherette – Platzanweiserin; to enfold – einhüllen; emperor – Kaiser; whisk – Quirl

I had really expected a little more fashion-consciousness from BJ, because I had a mega-cool **hairdo**. It took two hours out of my life. First of all I combed all my hair upwards to give it more **body**. I know from Linda that 'body' **is the in thing** this year, at least according to Serafina. And she should know. Then I coloured the tips in various different shades and threaded little flowers into it.

Even my mother thought it was **terrific**, telling me that I looked like a flower-power girl from the sixties. That should have **put me on my guard**. Whenever a mother thinks that an outfit or a hairdo is fantastic, you know that you must look absolutely untrendy.

But I had no time to do anything about it because Justus had already arrived.

Justus asked me why I had a Pumuckl hairdo, and I told him my mother had insisted on it. Otherwise she wouldn't have allowed me out of the house. Justus was surprised, but not too much so. He knows that we're not exactly a normal family.

Unfortunately something rather embarrassing also happened to me. When BJ came up to us I quickly put my hand in my pocket and **groped** for a peppermint, because fresh breath is an absolute must if you want someone to fall in love with you.

---

hairdo – Frisur; body – Volumen; to be the in thing – in sein; terrific – toll; to put sb on one's guard – jmd. stutzig machen; to grope – tasten

But in the **rush** I pulled out an old coat button instead of the peppermint. By the time I noticed my mistake, it was too late to spit it out. So I stood there with a coat button in my cheek. The stupid thing was that the button **pushed** my cheek **out** quite a long way and made talking difficult.

And when we all went off to get hot dogs, I had to try and chew the hot dog with a button in my cheek. Justus then made everything more embarrassing by asking me in front of all the others whether I wouldn't take the button out of my mouth at least to eat.

One thing about Justus gets on my nerves. Whenever his friends are about, he has to make some stupid comment so that everyone laughs at me. Otherwise he's really quite nice.

So I **mumbled** that my dentist had told me I should always do that when eating. To train my teeth. Justus said nothing more after that. BJ laughed out loud and told Justus that he had extremely poor taste.

I thought it was nice of BJ to **stand up for** me, but found this particular attempt had failed somewhat.

Could it be that Justus is even nicer than BJ?

---

rush – Hektik; to push out – ausbeulen; to mumble – nuscheln; to stand up for sb – jmd. in Schutz nehmen

By the way, Mother's new creation for me was a complete success. I knew it must be, because nobody commented on it. I was really grateful to my mother.

She said my hairdo had inspired her. When she saw it, she discarded the little cocktail dress she had made for me, stuck me in a pair of jeans, dug out an old T-shirt of hers with a 'Peace' symbol on the front and dropped an old sleeveless sheepskin jacket over my shoulders. That, she said, made me look really authentic.

I thought I looked as if I were on my way to try and stop a **consignment of atomic refuse**, but was happy that I didn't have to wear the cocktail dress.

Tuesday, 2nd June

Flippi is really impossible.

Today the mother of a boy in Flippi's class rang up to complain bitterly to my mother about Flippi.

It must have been something fairly serious because my mother was soon finding it hard to explain things. First of all, she tried to **deny** that Flippi was her daughter. But the other mother

---

consignment of atomic refuse – Atommülltransport;
to deny – abstreiten

wouldn't be **fobbed off** with that, so my mother ended up by saying: "I can't imagine Flippi doing that. That isn't her style at all."

Oh, anything is Flippi's style. My mother should **give in**. Whatever has happened, I'm fairly sure that Flippi is responsible.

As soon as she had finished the call, she stormed straight into Flippi's bedroom and asked her what she had done to Jan in her class who, incidentally, is a head taller than Flippi.

It **turned out** that Jan is in love with Flippi. So he walked up to her with a bar of chocolate and a bunch of **daisies** and asked Flippi if she wants to be his girlfriend.

And what does Flippi do?

She beat him up. Quite seriously. She **thrashed** the poor guy and told him that if he wanted her to go on playing football and gathering snails with him, he'd better forget such **drippy** nonsense. It was absolutely disgusting. Then she called him a flower-murderer and insisted that he should glue the flowers back on their **stalks**.

She took the bar of chocolate, of course, and told Jan that if he apologized for his embarrassing performance, she would be prepared to share it with him.

---

to fob off sb – jmd. abwimmeln; to give in – aufgeben;
to turn out – sich herausstellen; daisies – Gänseblümchen;
to thrash – verdreschen; drippy – schmalzig; stalk – Stängel

Although my mother could follow Flippi's argumentation, she told Flippi not to keep on beating up bigger boys. It was embarrassing for her to keep on getting complaints from the other mothers.

Flippi only said, **laconically**, that she couldn't promise not to, but she would do her best.

Incredible!

And I got into trouble in Second Grade because I told Katharina that I didn't want to be her friend. My mother thought that was extremely impolite. She forced me to apologize.

What my mother is doing is commonly known as 'measuring with two different yardsticks'. At least that's the polite way of putting it. The **unadulterated** truth is that the way she treats me is **outrageously** unjust.

No wonder I live my life on the **edge** of depression.

Wednesday afternoon, 3rd June

Somehow everything seems to be bewitched.

Justus wanted to go to the cinema with me. But he asked me not to chew buttons again and not to

---

laconically – ungerührt; unadulterated – unverblümt; outrageously – himmelschreiend; edge – Rand bother too much about my hairstyle. Otherwise we would only get into trouble with the people sitting behind us because they would constantly be asking me to take off my hat, as it was blocking their view. He said he could explain that to my mother if she **objected**.

First of all I wanted to go with him, but then I remembered that I had to stay by the telephone because I have put a spell on BJ to phone me and ask me out.

It's a pity, really.

So I told Justus I couldn't go. At first Justus said nothing, but then he asked me whether I had other plans and I told him I hadn't. I just had to stay at home and help my mother to **pickle gherkins**.

Goodness knows how I thought of that excuse! Nobody pickles gherkins nowadays. You buy them in jars at the supermarket.

I didn't mention waiting for BJ's phone call to Justus. I don't know why.

Anyway, in the afternoon I sat by the phone **cuddling** and cuddling the bear, and waiting. Until the phone finally rang. And who was it? You'd never guess: Serafina.

The bear is obviously slightly defective: I wish for a call from BJ and Serafina rings up.

---

to object – Einwände haben; to pickle gherkins – saure Gurken einmachen; to cuddle – fest drücken

Never mind. Serafina wanted to know whether I felt like coming down to the ice-cream parlour. BJ and the others would all be there.

Aha, I thought, the bear is still working. But **round corners**, unfortunately. Well, he's still only young and perhaps he doesn't get the spells to work out quite right.

So it's off to the ice-cream parlour and straight into BJ's arms!

Wednesday evening, 3rd June

It was a complete flop!

Nobody was there when I arrived at the ice-cream parlour. So I sat down and waited. Until BJ arrived. Of course he was too shy to sit down at my table. He went to the **counter**.

Serafina and her brother Justus were standing outside the ice-cream parlour. She was pointing **alternately** at me and at BJ. Justus only looked surprised at first, but then his expression changed to anger and he walked off.

Serafina smiled triumphantly, **strolled** calmly into the ice-cream parlour and went to stand beside BJ.

---

round corners – auf Umwegen; counter – Theke; alternately – abwechselnd; to stroll – schlendern

BJ saw her, looked at his watch and asked her where her brother was. Serafina shrugged her shoulders.

BJ was a bit annoyed and asked her what was going on. She had rung him and told him to come down to the ice-cream parlour because Justus had wanted to discuss something with him urgently. Serafina actually told him she didn't know where Justus was, but that BJ could buy her a Coke.

Somehow I had the feeling that something very **fishy** was going on and that it was all Serafina's doing. She's a stupid old **goat**, I thought to myself, and immediately had a suitable idea. I wished that she would bleat like a goat. I squeezed the bear and made my wish.

She'll really make a fool of herself in front of BJ, I thought, and **giggled** quietly.

But Serafina said nothing. She simply stared up **idolizingly** at BJ like a cow with a belly-ache.

BJ looked Serafina up and down, turned away from her and asked, as he walked out: "Is this another of your silly games?"

I had to prevent BJ from leaving the ice-cream parlour because of this stupid goat. So I jumped to my feet. Unfortunately a **loop** of my rucksack got caught in one of the chair legs. I lost balance, the

---

fishy – oberfaul; goat – Ziege; to giggle – kichern; idolizingly – anhimmelnd; loop – Schlaufe

chair fell over, I fell over and as I fell I pulled my full glass of Coke down with me.

BJ turned round, looked at me in astonishment, grinned and walked out.

And Serafina laughed out loud. It sounded just like the bleating of a goat.

It was only a pity that BJ was not there anymore to hear it.

Thursday, 4th June

Justus is angry with me.

He came up to me at school today and said that if I didn't want to go out with him I should say so **honestly** and not lie to him. He said he was grateful to his sister that she had opened his eyes for him.

Has he gone completely crazy? This is the first time he's said anything nice about his sister. But I'm afraid I don't know what he's talking about. And before I could ask him he had turned his back on me and walked away.

Hardly two seconds later BJ walked past and asked me: "Back on your feet again today, eh?"

Justus heard him and **gave him a black look**. The

---

honestly – ehrlich; to give sb a black look – jmd. böse anschauen

stupid expression on his face really spoilt BJ's attempted advance for me. I wonder whether BJ is really in love with me now?

Linda told me that Serafina had said that the cheekier boys behave, the more they are in love with a girl. BJ probably only has to realize this himself, then everything goes OK. But because he's a boy, this might take forever.

Boys are not exactly **quick on the uptake**. Especially not as far as their own feelings are concerned. We girls **cotton on** immediately. We know what's going on, we know our feelings. And the boys' feelings, too.

Somehow I feel a bit strange. As if I ought to **burst into tears**. But I don't, of course. And I won't miss Justus. Certainly not. Not on your life! I can **conquer** BJ without his help. After all, I have my bear and I can work magic.

---

to be quick on the uptake – eine rasche Auffassungsgabe haben; to cotton on – kapieren; to burst into tears – in Tränen ausbrechen; to conquer – erobern

Friday midday, 5th June

Everything's hunky-dory.

I've **virtually** conquered BJ. I shall be singing in his band!

BJ's band is participating in a talent competition the day after tomorrow. And Fee, the singer in the band, has **laryngitis**. Today I saw BJ's notice on the school notice board. Anyone interested in standing in as replacement singer for Fee should come along to **audition** this afternoon.

My bear certainly never runs out of ideas! I tell him I want to sing in BJ's band and he magics a sore throat for Fee. Actually that's a bit naughty of him. I feel really sorry for her. But we witches can't be softies!

Once upon a time, one of my colleagues even ate a small boy, didn't she? Or did Gretel manage to free Hansel in time? I think so.

Well – whatever. I have to **dash off** to the audition.

Incidentally, I couldn't care less whether Justus is angry with me or not.

---

virtually – so gut wie; laryngitis – Halsentzündung; audition – Vorsingen; to dash off – etwas schnell erledigen

Friday evening, 5th June

Wow! What a **stampede**! All the girls at our school were there!

When BJ and the boys from his band turned up, they first had to fight their way through a gigantic **concourse** of **would-be** girl singers. BJ was flustered, and said that it would take at least two weeks to audition them all. In fact, it took less time than that.

First of all he deselected all girls under twelve and over fifteen. They grumbled, of course, but finally left.

BJ and the boys then disappeared into the **rehearsal cellar** and Serafina attempted to get the other girls to go home by saying that it had already been decided that she should sing in the band. At which – unbelievably – most of them **actually** did wander off.

I didn't mind. There was no longer so much competition. Although that didn't matter, of course, because I had my bear with me and he is **responsible** for my super voice.

At last BJ called in the first candidate.

Serafina had elbowed her way to the front of the queue, of course, and insisted that she was first.

---

stampede – Menschenauflauf; concourse – Ansammlung; would-be – Möchtegern; rehearsal cellar – Probenkeller; actually – tatsächlich; responsible – zuständig

When she came out again she told the others that it was all over. BJ had decided to take her and the others could trot off home. And the handful of girls who hadn't believed her first time round now went away.

I didn't believe a word of it, of course, and stayed.

Until BJ stuck his head round the door. He was surprised that no one else was waiting, and waved me in.

I found it a bit silly that he actually asked me what my name was. Funny guy. He probably didn't want the other members of the band to know that he and I are friends. He thought they would otherwise certainly not have believed that he was **impartial**. OK – I played along with his little game.

I began to sing, putting my hand in my pocket and squeezing the bear hard all the time.

Just to be on the safe side and not to break the spell. I really sounded good. I'm not the worst singer, but with the bear to help me I was definitely **tops**.

Andi, one of the musicians, said I had a fairly useful voice, and Daniel commented approvingly that I was not as **prim** as the **bint** before me. (He meant Serafina. Haha!)

BJ shrugged his shoulders. If he only had to

---

impartial – unparteiisch; tops – spitze; prim – zickig; bint – Tussi choose between me and Justus's neurotic sister, he said, he would rather take me.

Then I had to promise him that I wouldn't do anything silly, that I wouldn't fall over on stage and drag the equipment down with me (he was referring to the incident in the ice-cream parlour) or try to sing with a button in my cheek. And I shouldn't do my hair like a broom again, either.

It didn't worry me that he spoke to me in such an unloving tone of voice, because I know from Linda that boys are unable to show their feelings.

We practised a bit more, then Serafina stuck her head round the door and asked whether I hadn't finished yet. She couldn't wait outside for ever.

I told her that she needn't wait any longer. She could go. BJ had chosen *me*.

Then she exploded.

She grabbed me by the **collar** and hissed at me: "You'll be sorry for this!"

To punish her, I made a wish that her hair should lose its colour, but she closed the door behind her so quickly that unfortunately nobody saw the change.

My mother was absolutely ecstatic when I told her about it. She was as pleased as if she herself had

---

collar – Kragen

been chosen to sing, and told me that she had always dreamed of becoming a singer.

But the worst part is that she has threatened to design and sew me an absolutely fantastic outfit.

Not again! What are shops for, anyway? She can be a real **spoilsport** sometimes!

Saturday, 6th June

Klarafina was sitting on her bench again today.

Strangely, she always gives me the feeling that we had agreed to meet and I had turned up late. She's such a **funny old bird**. But nice. Really nice.

The first thing she wanted was a report on how my life was getting on.

Well, all my news was good: everything is super good, couldn't be better. I told her how I had managed to become the singer in the school band, and Klarafina was very proud of me. She shared my joy.

Then she told me that I should use my powers in a sensible way.

I said I was doing that already.

But when I mentioned that I was in love with BJ and would soon be kissing him, she was horrified,

---

spoilsport – Spielverderber; funny old bird – kauzige Alte

saying emphatically that it would be better if I didn't.

I said nothing. But honestly – I only rarely allow my mother to forbid me anything. So why should I listen to the warnings of a dotty old lady? Even if she were the most experienced witch in the world!

Justus is still not talking to me – he **can take a running jump** as far as I'm concerned!

Monday, 8th June

It was absolutely fantastic!

My life is wonderful. I'm the star of the school. No wonder – after all, I *am* a witch!

Yesterday was the talent competition for young bands. I sang incredibly well. And nearly squeezed my poor bear to death! BJ told me to take my hand out of my jacket pocket, but I told him I had seen girl singers doing that on a music video. BJ then turned to the others and said he hoped Fee would soon be well again.

But that'll take longer than he thinks, because she's having her **tonsils** out. And so – hurrah, hur-

---

can take a running jump – kann einem gestohlen bleiben; tonsils – Rachenmandeln rah! – he has to take me to the recording studio with him. Because, of course, we won the talent competition!

I almost told BJ that I had arranged it with the help of my supernatural powers, but I think I'll let the band go on believing that they won it fair.

After our performance a lot of photos were taken. Of the band, of BJ and of me.

But at the critical moment, Flippi spoilt everything. The little **toad** was there, too, with her **dwarf**-friends.

I distinctly told my mother not to allow Flippi to bring them along. But she only said I shouldn't be so strict. After all, no one could stop Flippi's friends from going. It was an afternoon event and open to the general public, too.

That's how Flippi **did me out of** my kiss.

Everything got off to a perfect start.

The photographer wanted a photo of just BJ and me. BJ was supposed to put his arm round me, then we should both look at his camera over our shoulders and laugh.

That's exactly what we did. The photographer was very pleased. Then he asked BJ to kiss me. He said it would be a great photo.

---

toad – Kröte; dwarf – Zwerg; to do sb out of sth – jmd. um etwas bringen

I thought my heart would stop beating – I've reached the goal of my dreams. Everything will work out all right now. BJ will kiss me.

But BJ didn't think that was particularly cool. He tried to do a deal with the photographer. He said he would rather do something else. And I know why, of course. BJ would rather be alone with me for our first kiss, not in an unromantic atmosphere as this, with thousands of people **gawping at** us.

But the photographer wouldn't give in. He told BJ not to make such a fuss. Surely it wasn't his first kiss? Anyway, it was only for a photo, and BJ only had to pretend. The idea was to give the impression that BJ was totally happy with his new singer.

BJ finally gave in, leaned over me and, just before our lips touched (BJ's aim was not particularly good: if I hadn't turned my head at the right moment, his kiss would only have landed on my cheek – so he hasn't had a lot of practice) my stupid, **waste-of-space** sister called out: "Watch out, BJ. Jojo's got puberty, and that's **infectious**!"

BJ's head **jerked back** and he told the photographer that, after all, he'd rather just shake my hand. And that was the end of my kiss!

Flippi and the other dwarves laughed like drains.

---

to gawp at – anglotzen; waste-of-space – nichtsnutzig; infectious – ansteckend; to jerk back – zurückzucken

There and then I turned Flippi into a hamster, but I lost sight of her at the same moment. And no wonder in that crowd! One of the kiddies probably picked up Flippi and was pleased to have found a pet. **My pleasure** – any time!

Unfortunately, Flippi did in fact turn up at home later. As Flippi. No trace of fur or whiskers anywhere. Somehow my spells never seem to last very long.

Tuesday afternoon, 9th June

Klarafina doesn't understand me.

I went into town straight after school today and looked for Klarafina. Library, park, ice-cream parlour, the usual places. I was about to give up when I saw her sitting on a bench outside the old people's home. She became a bit **flustered** when she recognized me and walked to the park with me. To the bench where she usually waits for me.

I asked her whether she lived in the old people's home but she merely rolled her eyes and said I certainly had some strange ideas.

I told her what had happened right down to the

---

my pleasure – gern geschehen; flustered – nervös

smallest detail. The performance, my fantastic voice, that we had won first prize and also about Flippi and the kiss.

Klarafina listened to everything but seemed to be very worried by some of the things I told her. When I told her about the sad anticlimax of my first non-kiss, she was visibly relieved: "What a good thing Flippi was there," she sighed.

What a good thing??! Flippi is a catastrophe on two legs. But Klarafina shook her head and said I should be grateful to Flippi.

What?! Klarafina can never have had a little sister. Gratitude and little sisters are **mutually exclusive**! I tried to explain everything to Klarafina again in detail because I was certain she hadn't understood me properly. But she said I had been very lucky. Things might have gone badly wrong.

She has no idea! Things *did* go wrong, but Klarafina unfortunately doesn't understand this.

Maybe Klarafina isn't all too clear about the entire concept of love: first you fall in love, then you kiss. But she never wants to hear about love, she keeps on warning me about it.

I would really like to know why Klarafina is against my kissing BJ. Perhaps I should try to find Klarafina a husband, too. Once she has fallen in love, she'll know what I'm talking about. She'll cer-

---

to be mutually exclusive – sich gegenseitig ausschließen

tainly be grateful and won't make the sort of fuss my mother did.

When I suggested this to her, she came down to earth with a bump. "But Jojo, what a **preposterous** idea!"

I'm afraid I don't know what 'preposterous' means, so I'm not quite sure whether she was delighted or horrified.

Tuesday evening, 9th June

Wow! It nearly happened today: my first kiss.

We rehearsed all afternoon, and nothing embarrassing happened to me at all. Seriously. I was totally normal. BJ doesn't make me nearly as nervous as Justus does.

Justus – Bah! I won't waste another thought on *him*. Honestly. I **don't give a monkey's** what he does! He doesn't interest me at all.

During break he was standing around talking to some goat from another form in my grade. Linda was clinging to my arm all the time, sighing and talking about how **smashing** Justus looked and how

---

preposterous – hanebüchen; not to give a monkey's – sich einen Dreck drum scheren; smashing – umwerfend

swee-e-e-t he was. And she would love to be in love with him, but Serafina won't let her. And how lucky I was to have been out with him. And didn't I really find him smashing, too?

Justus – no, he's not my type at all.

That calmed Linda down, and she asked me for any tips I had about how she could get Justus to invite her to the cinema or buy her an ice-cream.

Tips from me! I ask you! But then I remembered that I was a witch who can do anything and who knows everything.

So I explained to her how you get a boy to fall in love with you: it all starts with the right outfit. You should style yourself to look at least three years older. It's also best to insist that you are considerably older. If anyone asks why you aren't in a higher grade at school, you say that you only started school at nine because your parents belong to a sect which forbids children to start school before they are nine. Then you look at the boy of your choice in a meaningful way. The best time to do this is when all his friends are present. As soon as his mates start to make jokes about him and start winding him up, you know you're on the right track. If he snaps at you, telling you to stop **goggling at** him in that stupid way, you can be certain that you've **hooked** him.

---

to goggle at sb – jmd. anstarren; to hook sb – jmd. an der Angel haben

You can, of course, simply walk up to the boy you find fantastic and ask him whether he would like to take you to the cinema. But that's far less thrilling.

Linda was completely fascinated by my lecture – so was I – and said it was a real pity that she couldn't be my best friend. But Serafina would never allow that.

Poor Linda.

Back to the rehearsal, and to my kiss that wasn't:

BJ was quite enthusiastic about me, and kept on praising me. When we had finally finished, it was already quite late and BJ offered to take me home.

Wow! BJ's taking me home! I was **over the moon**!

So there we were standing outside my front door and I was **frantically** trying to think what to say in such a situation. I thought back to all sorts of films that I've seen, but I couldn't think of a scene that fitted and the text of which I had learnt **by heart**.

So I drew circles on the pavement with the toe of my shoe. I'd read about that in a book. The girl was in love and the boy realized it when he saw her doing that.

But BJ didn't notice anything at first, although I had even begun to draw invisible hearts on the pavement with my foot.

---

to be over the moon – hin und weg sein;
frantically – krampfhaft; by heart – auswendig

BJ put his hand on my shoulder and said: "Well, then …"

What does "Well, then" mean in a situation like that? 'Well, then … Let's kiss'? – 'Well, then … Do you want to be my girlfriend?'? – "Well, then … Bye-bye!" is what BJ said.

Shit! That's not what I'd planned. I quickly said: "What do you really think of my voice?"

"It's great. Seriously, you're really great."

Me: "And what else?"

BJ: "What do you mean 'what else'?"

Me: "Well, 'what else' of course!"

Stupid dialogue! I've never heard or read anything as ridiculous as this.

BJ: "You've got a really great voice. And you're only thirteen."

I know what to say next: "I'll be fifteen soon."

BJ was quite astonished: "Really? When?"

As quietly as possible, I said: "In two years' time."

BJ laughed.

That was the time to make use of the bear. I had to do magic, I couldn't go on like this. I pressed the bear and wished for BJ to kiss me. I closed my eyes and waited.

Suddenly a window opened and I heard Flippi **bawl**: "Jojo, hurry up, it's bedtime. Children of your age should be in their beds at this time."

---

to bawl – plärren

I couldn't believe my ears! I opened my eyes.

BJ laughed, looked up at Flippi and said: "I think so, too. Her eyes were closed a moment ago." Then he patted me on the shoulder and walked off.

I couldn't believe it! Flippi had just spoilt my second first kiss!

Just you wait, Flippi. I'll **set** our mother **on you**!

Haven't seen Justus for two days.

Maybe he's ill? Actually, I don't give a monkey's, of course, but if it's something catching, **measles** or **chicken pox** or something like that, I ought to know. So that if I see a measle or a chicken pock on my nose, I don't go wild with joy in the belief that it's a pimple!

Wednesday afternoon, 10th June

Today was the most terrible day of my life. It's all over. BJ hates me. If he was ever in love with me, it's definitely all over now. Everything is so **dreadful**.

And it's all Flippi's fault. I'll never forgive her.

Last night, during supper, I said to my mother

---

to set sb on sb – jmd. auf jmd. hetzen; measles – Masern; chicken pox – Windpocken; dreadful – furchtbar

that I thought Flippi had serious psychological problems because she can't stand the sight of two people in love kissing and suffers from a **compulsion** to prevent it. I said that this was certainly because she was growing up without a father, and told my mother that it was high time she **looked after** her properly.

This is about the nastiest thing Flippi and I can do to each other: to make sure that our mother looks after us. Then she wants to spend a lot of time with us and even cooks us meals.

Cooking is always the first turn.

She goes into the kitchen and starts **raving on about** all the **special implements**. (We're talking about the wooden spoon and the **hand-whisk**.) In next to no time, the kitchen looks like a chemistry laboratory after an explosion.

Whatever she has mixed together and warmed up, she then calls a hot meal. But it's not always hot, because she hasn't mastered the use of the stove yet and is constantly turning on the wrong plates. After five minutes she says the food is ready – **patience** in the kitchen is not one of her strong points.

She sits down at the table with us and observes us

---

compulsion – Zwangsanwandlung; to look after sb – sich um jmd. kümmern; to rave on about sth – von etwas ganz begeistert sein; special implements – Spezialwerkzeuge; hand-whisk – Schneebesen; patience – Geduld

with excitement as we raise our forks to our lips. Then she wants to know what it tastes like.

It always tastes terrible, but we are **brave** and say "Great!". We know that she means well.

Sometimes we ask her why the sauce has such thick **lumps**, and she tells us that those aren't lumps but mushrooms. But the mushrooms are still in the tin, and the tin is standing beside the stove, unopened. My mother doesn't notice things like that. She had the idea to put some mushrooms in the gravy, and that is enough. In her opinion there are mushrooms in it. And we chew away at lumps of **flour**.

When we've finished, she tries the food herself, pulls a face and says: "Ugh! You can't possibly eat that!" She gets a bad conscience and invites us out for a pizza. That's the good part of the **special-care** programme.

But that's not the end of it: when we get home she wants to play party games with us.

That is very **strenuous**, because she is the worst winner in the world. Every time she wins she starts to **moan** that she didn't mean to win and was so sorry.

Then we have to console her for about two hours, and she only stops apologizing when we have

---

brave – tapfer; lump – Klumpen; flour – Mehl;
special-care – Sonderbetreuung; strenuous – anstrengend;
to moan – jammern

invented a rule according to which she hadn't actually won.

During these active 'caring-for-the-children' phases it is also a good idea not to bring friends home because our mother is completely **uninhibited** about applying her therapy to other children.

In any case, I don't have any friends any more. But Flippi has quite a band of followers. And in the meantime most of them ask Flippi before they come round whether it's really true that our mother won't be at home.

To put it **bluntly**: when our mother 'takes care' of us, it's a real punishment.

And that's exactly why I did it. Flippi had to be punished because she spoilt my first kiss.

The fact that I had turned her into a hamster was really meant as a punishment and warning for the future, but Flippi has learnt nothing from my spell. And, above all, Flippi even denied ever having been a hamster.

So I've set mother on her now.

Flippi was so annoyed with me as a result that she stole my bear.

She saw him and wanted to know where I'd got him from. I didn't tell her anything, of course. I just

---

to invent sth – etwas erfinden; uninhibited – hemmungslos; bluntly – unverblümt

told her to **toddle off** into her room and leave me in peace.

But she didn't go. She kept on getting on my nerves. I threatened to tell the bear to bite her on the nose if she went on sticking her nose into other people's business.

I should have known that that sort of thing doesn't work with Flippi. She probably thought: I'll really stick my nose in now, and **pinched** my bear. Out of my jacket pocket. And so that I wouldn't notice it straight away, she put something else into my pocket: a chocolate cake – without the packaging.

But I didn't know that when I set off for the recording studio.

So I walked into the recording studio, no prob, we're on. I took up my stance, put my hand in my jacket pocket and pressed as hard as I could. The chocolate cake, unfortunately. It crumbled.

I was so shocked that I screamed. When I took my sticky paw out of my pocket, BJ nearly flipped his lid. He said I wasn't here to perform one of my screwy **party pieces**, but to sing.

But how could I sing after that – without my bear? That wouldn't work. I'd sound like a chicken with a

---

to toddle off – abhauen; to pinch – stibitzen; party piece – Kunststückchen sore throat, but I couldn't tell BJ that. I went on screaming because I thought, of course, that I had squeezed the bear to a pulp. The thought almost made me **puke**.

BJ turned round and told me to disappear, saying to the **studio engineer** that they would come back when their normal singer was better again. And he **stressed** the word 'normal' as he gazed at me with a look that spoke volumes. So I went home.

That's how quickly a promising career can come to an end. So my singing days are over. What am I talking about singing for? My whole life is over.

I also hate Justus. I'll never speak a single word to him again. Linda told me, you see, that she'd seen him in the ice-cream parlour with two girls from Grade 8. Linda was quite **downhearted**. How can he do a thing like that to Linda? He's so rotten!

Wednesday evening, 10th June

Now I'm **in trouble with** my mother.

All because of Flippi.

When I got home from the recording studio I

---

to puke – kotzen; studio engineer – Aufnahmeleiter;
to stress – betonen; downhearted – geknickt;
to be in trouble with sb – mit jmd. Ärger haben

dashed into Flippi's room, knocked the little tick under her desk with a skilful blow and turned the room upside down in search of my bear. And how! – It was like a scene from a film. I **hurled** everything up to the ceiling.

Result – nix! So I grab Flippi by the collar and scream at her: "Where is he?! Come on, give him back!"

She plays the innocent and stares at me: "What do you mean?" But she knew exactly what I meant. I got even angrier and she called for her mummy, just **to be on the safe side**, and kicked me on the shin.

My mother came, saw and hissed: "What's going on here? Stop fighting immediately!"

But you can't just stop fighting just like that.

So she separated us and held us far apart. Flippi kept on trying to hit me, screaming: "It's always my fault when she can't find something!"

"Because you're always pinching my things. Now give me my bear back!"

My mother let go of Flippi and dragged me to the door. Then what I really hate happened: "Jojo, you're the eldest and **have more sense** ..."

"But she took my bear," I complained. "I know she did and I need him urgently!"

---

to hurl – schleudern; to be on the safe side – sicherheitshalber; to have more sense – vernünftiger sein

To which my mother replied in her typical 'reproachful-mother' tone. "But Jojo, how on earth can you need a bear 'urgently'? Flippi, have you got it?"

"No-o-o," said Flippi **feigning** injured innocence.

And my mother believed her. That can't be true! I made a weak attempt: "But …"

That was enough for my mother: "Jojo, I don't want to hear any more about it. I've got work to do." **Muttering to herself**, she pushed me through the doorway.

Just you wait, Flippi! My revenge will be terrible. And I know what I'm going to do already. Something **significant**. Flippi must learn to stay in her room and not nose around in my things! I'll smear super-glue on her desk chair, and when she sits down on it she'll stay where she is. For a very long time.

Sunday, 14th June

My mother is still **cross**. Really, genuinely angry. She's **fed up with** us. She didn't think much of my idea with the glue. The symbolism of my gesture

---

to feign – vortäuschen; to mutter to oneself – vor sich hin grummeln; significant – bedeutungsvoll; cross – sauer; to be fed up with – die Nase voll haben von

was unclear to her, she just thought it was completely **potty**. She's still thinking about how best to punish me.

Oops!

She's screaming at me again to switch my light off. I'd better do just that.

Monday, 15th June

You have to have seen it to believe it. It was like this: we're sitting at the breakfast table. My mother is making our school sandwiches. She's already made seven sandwiches. My mother is cross. She keeps on making sandwiches. Icy silence. Even Flippi is quiet.

I cautiously attempt conversation: "Mummy, I only wanted …"

My mother interrupts me immediately: "There's no explanation for it. You're too old to do something so stupid. What on earth were you thinking about?"

"I was thinking …"

My mother interrupts me. "Be quiet! I don't want to hear another word."

How about that? Typical of all mums: they ask a

---

potty – durchgeknallt

question, and when you start to answer it, they say: "Be quiet."

She goes on angrily making sandwiches. This is the tenth, because she isn't watching what she's doing.

Flippi gives me a sign, makes a **tormented** face because our mother has finished another sandwich and shows no sign of stopping.

I just shrug my shoulders.

My mother looks at me. "I still can't believe it. Why do you do things like that?"

I cautiously try again: "But Mummy …"

She lifts a hand: "Say nothing!"

Flippi **butts in**: "Mummy, Jojo only wants to tell you that you're putting butter on the twelfth sandwich. I could feed my entire class with that pile!"

My mother hisses at Flippi: "And you be quiet, too."

Then she looks at the sandwiches, puts the knife down and says: "I really am far too nice to you."

She gathers the sandwiches and stacks them on her plate. "Make your own sandwiches. I'll eat these!" She takes a hearty bite and wanders off into her workroom with the plate in the other hand.

How can we children turn out right with **role-models** like that?

---

tormented – gequält; to butt in – sich einmischen; role-model – Vorbild

Flippi then **penitently** pushed the bear across the table to me and I was too dejected to give her a **clip on the ear**.

Strange. I miss Justus. What a pity that we're not friends any more. Not that I'm in love with him or anything like that. It's just that … oh, hell, I don't know. There's nothing much wrong with him. He's real cool, I suppose. I mean good-cool, not stupid-cool like most of them.

Wednesday, 17th June

I'll **tar and feather** Flippi! She's done just about the most **embarrassing** thing possible. She's written Justus a love letter. In my name! And I had no idea.

It all happened like this: I was lying on my bed this afternoon in a bad mood, wishing that BJ would phone me. But nothing happened. I don't know what's wrong with my bear.

The doorbell rang and a few moments later my mother poked her head round the door: "Jojo, you have a visitor."

---

penitently – reumütig; clip on the ear – Ohrfeige; to tar and feather – teeren und federn; embarrassing – peinlich

Wow! BJ's come round to see me! Fantastic, I thought.

I jumped up, looked around my room in panic, quickly hid the bear under the **bedspread** and pushed everything that looked too much like a little girl's stuff under the bed.

Then I draped myself **casually** and still a little out of breath across my bed, picked up a book and pretended that I was reading. Unfortunately I didn't realize that I was holding the book upside down.

The door opens and I glance up from my book.

But it wasn't BJ standing in the doorway, but Justus. I was completely confused and could only say: "Oh, it's you."

Justus was slightly **offended**: "Of course. Were you expecting someone else?"

Well, actually I was. I had definitely told the bear that I wanted BJ.

But then I noticed that I was really happy to see Justus. Honestly. So I quickly replied: "No-o-o, I was just thinking aloud. So what are you doing here?"

Justus didn't reply. He only pointed to my book and said: "Are you practising reading on your head?"

---

bedspread – Tagesdecke; casually – lässig;
offended – gekränkt

Embarrassing. "Of course," I replied. "It's training for logical thinking."

Justus didn't believe a word of it. Not even when I told him that I had discovered this fact in a book entitled 'Learning Logic Made Easy' by Professor Hans-Joachim Winzelpütz, Ph.D.

I got up, put the book away and looked at Justus.

Justus got a bit **embarrassed**. Quite seriously, I've never seen him like that before.

Then he mumbled: "Thank you for your letter."

Letter? What letter?

I must have asked the question out loud, because Justus replied: "Your letter. The one your little sister gave me."

"That toad gave you a letter!"

Justus was a bit confused. "Yes. With best wishes from you. Your name was at the bottom, too."

"Good heavens!" I couldn't think of anything else to say. Flippi certainly didn't do it to do me a favour. She wanted to embarrass me. Just to be on the safe side, I told Justus that I had nothing to do with the letter. It was probably my loopy little sister who had written it.

Justus was obviously disappointed: "I see. So not one word of what she wrote is true?"

"Not one word."

"Pity!" Justus didn't look very happy.

---

embarrassed – verlegen

I felt sorry I'd said what I said, because I was curious to know what was in the letter.

But Justus was not to be led into my little **trap**. "It doesn't matter. You didn't write it after all."

Shit! I would really like to have known what was in it, because Justus wasn't at all angry. Perhaps it was a nice letter.

Must have been a nice letter, because Justus suddenly held out a present for me. "Here. You can have it anyway."

I was completely **flabbergasted**. My first present from a boy!

I tore the package open and went red as a **beetroot**.

It was a wristwatch. Pink with hearts on it. It's so-o-o-o sweet! I've always wanted one just like it. Justus is so-o-o-o nice. What on earth could have been in that letter?

When Justus had gone, I wondered whether I should really punish Flippi. Her dotty letter has, so to speak, brought Justus and me together again. What do I mean: 'brought us together again'? We're talking to one another again, because I was able to explain the ice-cream parlour **incident** to Justus. He understood immediately, saying it was typical of Serafina to **hatch plots**, to scheme and

---

trap – Falle; flabbergasted – von den Socken;
beetroot – rote Bete; incident – Vorfall; to hatch a plot – etwas aushecken

that sort of thing. So Justus wasn't cross with me about that any more.

And then Justus wanted to know whether it was true that I was in love with BJ. Oooh, what an embarrassing question! I told him that I was in love with nobody. My mother had forbidden me to fall in love. She said it was unhealthy.

Justus gave me a pitying look: "Your mother is a bit **peculiar**, isn't she?"

I could only agree with him.

It could be that Flippi is perhaps quite a nice girl after all. Because I called on her immediately and asked her why she had written Justus a letter in my name. She had the nerve to say that she had been sorry to see how **sad** I had been recently and that she had thought it might be because I haven't been seeing Justus lately. So she had written him a love letter.

I was quite **touched**. I cuddled her and told her that she had done wrong, even if it was right. But that only confused her. But I couldn't find a better way of explaining things.

And that almost might have been the first day we hadn't had an argument.

But then she said: "To be on the safe side, I wrote a letter to BJ, too."

She probably thought I would praise and cuddle

---

peculiar – merkwürdig; sad – traurig; touched – gerührt

her the more, and was terribly shocked when, instead, I began to shake her and scream at her, calling her the rottenest sister in the world.

Flippi screamed back that I ought to have an anti-puberty **jab** and that it was impossible to live with me. Then she kicked me on the shin and ran off.

I've been embarrassed right down to my toenails! What on earth is BJ expected to think of me? I can never go to school again. I can't ever show my face there.

My life is **in ruins**.

I'll have to leave school. At the age of thirteen. What is to become of me? I mean **vocationally**, for instance. No school-leaving certificate. Breaking off my education in the middle of seventh grade? What will the **careers officer** at the **Jobcentre** say about that? What sort of profession does that qualify me for?

I'm afraid it's not even good enough to qualify me for the job of **Federal Chancelloress**. That was my alternative if I failed to make a career as a singer. And that career **went down the pan** thanks to the chocolate cake. How can life go on after this?

I cried a little and talked to the bear about my suf-

---

jab – Impfung; to be in ruins – ruiniert sein; vocationally – beruflich; careers officer – Berufsberater; Jobcentre – Arbeitsamt; Federal Chancelloress – Bundeskanzlerin; to go down the pan – den Bach runtergehen

ferings. Then I remembered that I'm a witch and have absolutely no reason to **moan**. I can't understand why I keep on forgetting that.

Thursday, 18th June

Yet another problem. Not a day goes by without stress! I had arranged to meet Justus at the ice-cream parlour. On my way there I saw Klarafina sitting on the park bench. So of course I first went over to Klarafina. I was already a bit late, but I thought that Justus would wait for me.

Klarafina was sitting there so alone, and I had the feeling that I should make sure she was OK.

She wasn't in her usual good mood and told me reproachfully that I was late. I thought she meant my date with Justus and was surprised that she knew anything about it. So I said: "Well, only a couple of minutes."

She asked me what I meant by minutes and told me she'd been waiting for me for three hours. I said that was impossible, that I knew nothing about it.

Klarafina gave a loud sigh and said she had sent me a telepathic message. She asked me if I hadn't received it.

---

to moan – jammern

Interesting. It was completely new to me that witches can communicate via **thought transfer**. But I didn't want to admit it. It might be that every normal witch knows that sort of thing automatically and that I'm maybe only a second-class witch. I mean now and again my spells somehow go wrong. And until I know whether it's the bear's fault or mine, I'd better keep my mouth shut.

So I just said I hadn't received any messages. Klarafina was still looking at me a little reproachfully, but finally told me to sit down and gave me an ice-cream.

We chatted quite **cosily** until she suddenly got **restless**. When I asked her what the matter was, she told me she was just receiving a message. But there was some kind of **interference** and she would have to change her position **briefly**. She said it, pushed her ice-cream sundae into my hand and was gone. But Mathilde was still sitting next to me – her handbag.

I felt sorry for Mathilde and talked to her a bit so that she wouldn't miss Klarafina so much.

Suddenly I heard a voice behind me: "Hey, Jojo! Where've you been? We had a date."

Justus was standing behind me. What a shock I got! And before I could say anything, he asked me: "Are you talking to yourself?"

---

thought transfer – Gedankenübertragung;
cosily – gemütlich; restless – unruhig; interference – Funkstörung; briefly – kurzfristig

"No," I said, but then I realized that perhaps he had heard me talking to Mathilde, so I quickly corrected myself: "Yes."

Justus came round the bench and sat down beside me. Then he saw the two ice-cream sundaes in my hands and I could see the surprise in his look.

I pushed one of them into his hand. "Here. This is for you. I thought we'd eat our ice-cream in the park."

He took the sundae with a confused look but **nevertheless** started to eat it.

Now I had to **straighten him out** about the **soliloquies**, so I told him I was practising **ventriloquism** for the school festival.

"Which school festival?" asked Justus.

"Well, it doesn't matter for which one. We'll certainly have another school festival some time, and by then I'll really be in practice."

In order to make sure that he believed me, I picked a daisy, held it by the stalk and pushed it in front of Justus's face.

I moved it up and down like a puppet and, disguising my voice and without moving my lips, said: "Hello, Justus. I'm Gloria the Daisy."

That wasn't a very good idea, because Justus

---

nevertheless – nichtsdestotrotz; to straighten sb out – jmd. etwas erklären; soliloquy – Selbstgespräch; ventriloquism – Bauchreden looked at me as if I'd just gone crazy, shrugged his shoulders and said: "You're an **offbeat** girl all right."

I threw Gloria over my shoulder and concentrated on eating my ice-cream once more.

Then I thought of a good way to **distract** him. "The watch you gave me is really smashing, by the way."

That embarrassed Justus a little. I could tell, because he made a casual movement with his spoon full of ice-cream which **catapulted** the ice-cream in a sweeping movement from the spoon. It landed on a **blackbird**. This was quite embarrassing for Justus.

Then, just to confirm my compliment and to distract attention from Justus's **clumsiness**, I looked at my pink watch. Unfortunately I had forgotten that I was still holding the sundae cup. Splosh! The ice-cream landed on my trousers.

Justus then clumsily tried to wipe the ice-cream off my trousers.

After that neither of us really knew what to say to one another, and we had eaten the ice-cream anyway.

Then Klarafina came back.

She picked up her handbag and told her: "So this

---

offbeat – unkonventionell; to distract – ablenken;
to catapult – schleudern; blackbird – Amsel; clumsiness – Ungeschicklichkeit

is where I left you!" Then she saw the empty sundae cups, looked at me, then at Mathilde again. She opened the handbag, looked inside it and, **wrinkling her brow**, said to me: "Those were my two last ones." With a sigh she added that she had an **emergency** to attend to and that we would have to meet another time. Off she trotted.

Justus immediately wanted to know, of course, who she was and what she had meant, and whether I had eaten the old lady's ice-cream.

I said that I hadn't – *he* had!

Justus told me he had only taken it because he had thought it was my ice-cream.

"Oh," I said. "So you think I would sit here alone in the park with two ice-cream sundaes?"

When I looked at Justus, I noticed that our conversation was somehow going wrong, but I didn't exactly know how to stop it. Justus then simply said that nothing about me surprised him.

I didn't know what to say and asked him why he was **spying on me**.

He got cross and said I was completely crackers.

Then I offered to give him his watch back.

He stood up and told me to keep it, saying that then at least something about me would be ticking correctly, and off he went.

---

wrinkling her brow – stirnrunzeln; emergency – Notfall; to spy on sb – jmd. nachspionieren

Now I don't really know what will happen with Justus and me. Are we still talking to each other? Or aren't we? Do I have to apologize? Or does he? Does this officially count as an **argument**? If it does, does it mean that we aren't friends any more?"

In actual fact, this was our second argument, if you count the ice-cream parlour episode.

Then I would, of course, have to know how often you can have an argument without a friendship actually falling apart. Is there a limit – three times or ten times, then it's all over?

I'll wait and see. If necessary, Flippi can write him another letter. Which reminds me: I still don't know what was in the first letter.

First of all, Flippi said she couldn't remember. Then, when we had our little disagreement, she said, cheekily, that she had copied a recipe for **meatballs in caper sauce**.

If that's right, it must be Justus's **favourite dish**, otherwise he wouldn't have given me a watch.

---

argument – Streit; in actual fact – genau genommen; meatballs in caper sauce – Königsberger Klopse; favourite dish – Lieblingsessen

Monday, 22nd June

The drama goes on and on.

I really didn't think that things could get worse, but they did. Now the ultimate catastrophe is ready to explode. All because of a fashion trend.

Everybody at school wears the same jacket.

It's not that we have to wear school uniform. No. But everyone **who thinks himself anyone** is wearing a special kind of worn, **frayed** jeans jacket with Japanese writing on the back. Nobody has any idea what the writing means. I expect that it's just been copied from a Japanese menu and means 'escalope of veal with chips and mayonnaise', only in Japanese.

A couple of hopeless romantics are of the opinion that it is an old Japanese **blessing** that goes: 'May, today and every day, the sun show you the way to walk life's path **in cheerfulness and gaiety**.'

The boys insist that it means: 'Death to the **traitor**.' It doesn't really matter. Anyway, almost everyone at school is wearing the same kind of jacket.

That's the only way it could have happened. And I only noticed it when I got home. I put on some-

---

to think oneself anyone – etwas auf sich halten; frayed – ausgefranst; blessing – Segensspruch; in cheerfulness and gaiety – heiter und beschwingt; traitor – Verräter

one else's jacket. The jacket with the bear in it!!! My bear is gone!

And who's got him? Serafina.

Serafina of all people! I know it's her because the jacket which I was wearing had a letter from Linda to Serafina in the pocket. She wrote her that she had got a sweet new pink patent-leather belt and asked her whether she could bring it to show Serafina and whether Serafina would like to wear it. She hadn't worn it yet because she knows that Serafina doesn't like used things.

When I read things like that, it makes me want to throw up. But why am I worrying about Linda when my world is coming to an end and I shall most probably die of **grief**.

The perfect catastrophe! Serafina will find the bear and certainly discover his secret. Then Serafina will be able to do magic. Of all people in the world she ought to be the last to be allowed to cast spells. Then everybody will have to look out. She will turn us all into toads and **warthogs**. Serafina – a witch!!!

That will be the end for me. My **heyday** will be over. 'Go to jail. Do not pass "Start". Do not collect two thousand Euros.' I'm ruined.

Who says that life is a **roller-coaster**? Nonsense –

---

grief – Kummer; warthog – Warzenschwein;
heyday – Glanzzeit; roller-coaster – Berg- und Talbahn

life is a **ski-jump**, and just as you're about to jump, they **whip** your skis **away**.

And I did so enjoy being a witch. Everything was finally beginning to work out in my life.

Tuesday, 23rd June

Yes, it's all over with me.

Serafina can cast spells. I'm sure of it. Yesterday in the playground, BJ came up to her and gave her a book. He said it was for her brother, but I'm sure he must have put a love letter to Serafina inside it.

My BJ spell is probably still working and the bear hasn't noticed that he has a new owner. He is now making sure that Serafina gets BJ.

She strolled over to me and said in her sugar-sweet way: "Oh, Joho baby, I've got a suggestion about how you can make yourself more attractive. Put a **bag** over your head!"

Then she **breezed off**, the chickens giggling behind her.

I couldn't think of anything to say now that all my strength as a witch is gone, and Serafina has got it.

It's really terrible.

---

ski-jump – Sprungschanze; to whip away – wegreißen; bag – Tüte; to breeze off – abrauschen

Without my powers as a witch I am lost. Now I am powerless and have to let her do anything she wants to me, like all the other chickens.

In my despair I even asked Flippi for her advice. I've never done that before. Flippi just asked me in a matter-of-fact tone why I didn't simply tell Serafina that we had taken each other's jacket by mistake and ask her to **swap**.

Sometimes Flippi makes me really angry.

Especially when she's right.

I simply hadn't thought of that. I panicked so badly because I was suddenly no longer a witch that I can't even think of the simplest things.

But I couldn't tell Flippi that.

Flippi looked at me, shook her head and asked me if puberty had made my brain stop functioning.

I said she was a stupid **twit**, told her to leave me alone and to disappear out of my room.

But unfortunately I was in *her* room, so I had to **meekly** disappear myself.

It's not easy with Flippi when we have a quarrel. I'm a good five years older than her, but the age difference doesn't help me when we're quarrelling. It's awful. You can't win an argument against her. Not even my mother can.

---

to swap – tauschen; twit – Trottel; meekly – kleinlaut

This morning Flippi asked my mother if she could **repaint** her room. My mother said no.

This lunch-time, Flippi started to move the furniture in her room to the middle, covering it with old cloths.

My mother asked her what she thought she was doing, and Flippi said: "I'm getting everything ready because I'm going to paint my room."

My mother wanted to know whether Flippi had beans in her ear-holes, saying she hadn't given Flippi **permission** to paint her room.

To which Flippi replied, with perfect coolness: "I know. I'm not actually painting it yet. But if you change your mind, I can start straight away."

My mother said she wasn't going to change her mind, and walked out of the room.

In the evening, Flippi began to paint.

I asked her whether our mother had changed her mind. Flippi said no. But she certainly would when she saw the newly-painted bedroom.

Can you believe it?! Where does this dwarf get the nerve for a trick like that? And the worst thing is, she always gets away with it! She'll get away with this painting **lark**, too, I'm quite certain of it.

At first my mother won't be able to believe her eyes, then she'll quickly grab one of her clever

---

repaint – neu anstreichen; permission – Erlaubnis; lark – Zeug 'how-to-bring-up-children' manuals and begin wildly **leafing through** it. After that she will **assert** that, basically, this is one quality that will be very useful to Flippi in later life. In this case 'quality' means: Flippi's habit of ignoring my mother's orders.

That woman is quite impossible, isn't she?

Nevertheless, I'm going to follow Flippi's advice: I'll simply exchange my jacket.

Wednesday, 24th June

Serafina wasn't wearing the jacket.

Impossible! Normally we all wear our jackets every day. Our mothers have been strictly **forbidden** to wash the jackets. And if they insist, they have to wash them at night. If they can't get the jacket dry by the following morning, we put our jackets on wet. Just to teach our mothers a lesson!

Rumour has it that some mothers have **clandestinely** bought a second jacket so that nobody notices if they occasionally wash the first.

So I can't understand why Serafina turned up

---

to leaf through – durchblättern; to assert – versichern; forbidden – verboten; clandestinely – heimlich

without a jacket. Maybe she has made it **invisible** just to annoy me.

It's really awful. Serafina is already **better off** than most of us, and now she's a witch as well.

Life is unjust. In every **respect**.

Quite apart from which, I missed a natural catastrophe at home today. My mother flipped her lid when she saw Flippi's room. She **went** absolutely **bananas**. She raged, she screamed, she threatened and even cursed.

For the first time in her life she reacted like a normal mother – and I missed it! Shit!

But Flippi had really taken things a bit too far. Flippi wanted a cave, one just like the Flintstones have.

Actually it really was high time that Flippi's room was re-papered and painted. For in the course of time, Flippi had scribbled moustaches on all the sweet little princesses dancing **ring-a-ring-o'-roses** across her wallpaper, blacked out some of their teeth or drawn **patches** over their eyes. And she had painted monsters and disgusting animals everywhere.

Scary! So much so that if I had to go into Flippi's

---

invisible – unsichtbar; to be better off – es besser haben; respect – Hinsicht; to go bananas – durchdrehen; ring-a-ring-o'-roses – Ringelreihen; patch – Augenklappe

room just before going to bed, I always had nightmares.

So she had decided to re-create the **Flintstones'** cave and began to paint the walls a **boggy** greyish-brown.

She really had no choice in the selection of colour, because our mother hadn't allowed her to buy paint. So Flippi simply mixed up all the paint leftovers which she found in the cellar.

Of course she hasn't had very much painting practice, so one or two strokes went onto the **skirting**. Because she has a practical nature, Flippi thought: OK, so I'll paint the skirting brown, too.

A bit of paint got onto the door **frame** and Flippi thought: OK, so I'll paint the door frame brown, too.

While she was doing that, some paint got onto the door, and Flippi thought: OK, so I'll paint the door brown, too.

And it was the same with the door handle, the window and so on.

To cut a long story short: the whole room is brown. Walls, ceiling, door, the window – including the **panes** – and even the carpet: everything has been painted brown. Because a bit of paint dripped on the carpet …

Flintstones – Familie Feuerstein; boggy – schlammig; skirting – Fußbodenleiste; frame – Rahmen; pane – Scheibe

It's **ghastly**, it really is!

Even if Flippi were my favourite sister, that's what I'd say.

In dictatorships, this room would be used for **interrogations**. Everyone would immediately confess to anything just to get out of the room quickly.

Flippi was very satisfied with her work, but she was the only one.

My mother shouted so much that she couldn't speak for two hours afterwards. And when her voice had more or less recovered, she **hoarsely** whispered to Flippi that Flippi should leave her room immediately and **move in** with me.

How about that? Now I get punished, too!

My mother tried to find a painter and decorator who could **make good the damage**.

Three different decorators were there. All three **refused** to restore this room to its original condition.

Then Flippi had an idea. "Why don't you ask Oskar Hase?"

Oskar also works at the theatre. He paints the **scenery**. We know him quite well. He used to visit us often.

My mother and he had to **collaborate**. Sometime

---

ghastly – grauenhaft; interrogation – Verhör; hoarsely – heiser; to move in – einziehen; to make good the damage – den Schaden beheben; to refuse – sich weigern; scenery – Kulisse; to collaborate – zusammenarbeiten

at his place, usually at ours. Rarely at the theatre, but never mind.

One day he stopped coming. I mean, to tell the truth, he kept on phoning but every time my mother said she didn't have time. I ask you! Either they have to work together or they don't. She can't just say she doesn't have time. But that's my mother all over.

Oskar was really great. He was always on our side, and the three of us **drove** my mother **to the edge of madness**. He really had even worse ideas than Flippi. My mother moaned, asking what she had done wrong in her **former life** to be punished by being surrounded by people like us.

Anyway, Oskar stopped coming, and when we asked about him my mother always got into a bad mood.

And when Flippi mentioned Oskar now, our mother immediately hissed that it was out of the question. She said she was fed up with Flippi's good ideas. We would see what would happen. Flippi should **keep a low profile** for the next future.

But Flippi has this 'quality' (disobedience, I mean). She ran straight off to the theatre and began **negotiations** with Oskar.

---

to drive sb at the edge of madness – jmd. an den Rand des Wahnsinns treiben; former life – früheres Leben;
to keep a low profile – sich zurückhalten; negotiations – Verhandlungen

He was a bit undecided and asked Flippi twice if it was really OK from our mother's point of view.

Flippi said of course it was. Our mother had sent her.

Then Oskar broke into a broad smile and promised to **pop in** tomorrow.

Sometimes I envy Flippi her nerves.

She's just dropped off to sleep in the middle of the story she was telling me. And she looks really sweet.

Spending a couple of nights with her in the same room isn't so bad after all.

All this stress with Flippi has almost made he forget my own drama.

I don't dare tell Klarafina about what's happened to the bear. She'll certainly think I was completely **irresponsible**. I might possibly be excluded from the witches' club now that I've lost my **magic charm**. I think it's really rotten: either I can't get into a club or if I do, I **get booted out** again in seconds flat! What is to become of me? I'm the worst witch in the world. No – I'm not even a witch any more!

---

to pop in – vorbeikommen; irresponsible – unverantwortlich; magic charm – Zaubergegenstand; to get booted out – rausgeschmissen werden

Thursday, 25th June

When I got home today, Oskar was already there.

I was really pleased to see him.

My mother was standing there, red in the face, saying that it was all a misunderstanding. She said she didn't need any help, everything was fine, and that he could go now. But Oskar was **suspicious** and didn't look as if he was going to leave. He looked at Flippi with a question in his eyes.

Then Flippi dragged him into her room and whispered that my mother had re-painted her room. She asked him whether he didn't think this was a call for help.

Oskar was deeply moved and **promised faithfully** firstly to do something about the room and secondly to do something about our mother.

Then I came to Flippi's assistance by telling Oskar he shouldn't show any reaction if our mother said that this was all Flippi's work. If she wanted to believe that, we should let her believe it.

But by then my mother was already standing in the doorway, saying in a meek voice that it might, after all, be a good idea to re-paint the room. Flippi had …

But Oskar didn't even let her finish her sentence.

---

suspicious – misstrauisch; to promise faithfully – hoch und heilig versprechen

He put his arm consolingly around her shoulders and told her not to worry. He would **put everything right**. Then he asked her if she wouldn't like to go out this evening for a pizza with him and **get it all off her chest**. It might be a little too much to take over full responsibility for two children all on her own.

My mother said he was probably right. But when Oskar looked at her so sweetly, she blushed and said she didn't have time to go out for a meal with him.

My mother might possibly have an Oskar allergy. I know all about that from me and Justus.

Oskar looked at my mother full of understanding and said that was OK. He promised to come back tomorrow evening and start to put Flippi's room back into order.

My mother was a little **confused**. So confused that, when Oskar had gone, she even forgot to shout at Flippi.

---

to put everything right – alles in Ordnung bringen;
to get sth off one's chest – sich etwas von der Seele reden;
confused – verwirrt

Friday midday, 26th June

I want my bear back!

Even if he couldn't cast spells, I'd still want him back. He was so sweet. I must get him back.

But first of all I have to know whether the bear is still in my jacket.

Justus must help me. He must find out why Serafina no longer wears the jacket and where she has hidden it. Maybe it's only invisible at school and you can see it again when she gets home.

The only thing is that I don't really know how to explain the situation to Justus. I'd better tell him that we took each other's jacket **by mistake**. I'll give him Serafina's and ask him to bring me mine back.

If I told him about the bear, he'd only get confused.

Most things confuse him. At least when it's me who's explaining them!

---

by mistake – aus Versehen

Friday evening, 26th June

Justus will do it!

It was all quite easy. I told him without making a big fuss and he said that wasn't a problem.

Then I realized that we were really not on speaking terms after our argument. And I mumbled quietly: "Sorry about what happened in the park."

He looked at me and said: "That's OK. You're just a bit **loopy**, that's all."

I looked at him questioningly, and he hurriedly said that he found it cool.

Hey! Justus thinks I'm cool.

I'm cool! At last!

I've been waiting so long to hear that!

Ever since I was at kindergarten I've been trying to be one of the cool kids. In those days all cool kids had pets. Tobias had a guinea pig. Janina had a hamster and Mara even had a dog. Of course I wanted to have a pet, too.

But my mother said no.

So I caught two wild animals and **tamed** them. What else could I do? They were called Pixie and Dixie. And they were so sweet and did everything I told them to.

I talked about them a lot at kindergarten, and

---

loopy – abgedreht; to tame – zähmen

everybody **envied** me. Tobias and Mara came to my house one day to see Pixie and Dixie.

I let them loose to show Tobias and Mara the tricks I had taught them. Just at that moment my mother happened to come into the room and killed Pixie and Dixie with the **fly-swatter**. Tobias and Mara didn't understand me and said that two stupid **flies** were not real pets. And my mother said they were quite right, too.

Tobias and Mara never came round to play again, and they told everyone at the kindergarten about my two pet flies. Everybody laughed at me.

Never before in my life has anyone said I was cool. So I need to get my bear back quickly so that I can stay cool.

I've made a start. I've given Justus Serafina's jacket and he's trotted off home with it.

Saturday midday, 27th June

Justus came a while ago and brought me my jacket. That took a **load of my mind**. But then it fell back again! The bear was not in my jacket.

I was so shocked I began to cry. Justus was quite

---

to envy – beneiden; fly-swatter – Fliegenpatsche; fly – Fliege; sth takes a load of one's mind – jmd. fällt ein Stein vom Herzen

confused. It was only with difficulty that I managed to tell him that my bear was missing. My sweet little favourite bear. And that I had only wanted the jacket back because of the bear. Because he is my … lucky bear.

Justus then searched the jacket pockets again and found one of BJ's exercise books.

I began **sobbing** even harder. If BJ keeps his exercise books in Serafina's jacket, I no longer have any chance! She must have discovered the bear and realized that he has magic powers. The next moment she put a spell on BJ to make him fall in love with her. But I didn't tell Justus that.

Justus drew another conclusion from the presence of the exercise book: it's BJ's jacket.

I found that so fantastic that I immediately put the jacket on.

Justus explained everything to me. Yesterday BJ had been round at his house and had probably mistaken his jacket for Serafina's, or rather for my jacket. So Serafina now has her own jacket back, and BJ and I are the ones with the **switched** jackets.

That consoled me: BJ is now wearing my jacket and I'm wearing his. Like a real pair of **love-birds**. That's wonderful. I wonder if the bear planned it all?

---

to sob – schluchzen; switched – vertauscht;
love-birds – Turteltauben

But that also means that BJ now has the magic bear.

I wonder if the magic works for boys? Whether BJ is now a witch?

Justus told me to give him BJ's jacket and he'd get me mine back.

When I refused to take the jacket off, he looked at me in a funny way and asked me whether I was sure I wasn't in love with BJ.

"Absolutely sure," I lied.

That was clearly a **white lie**. I can't be punished for it.

In all probability, you don't get punished for lying anyway. It's only a story my mother invented. Because the punishments she told me about were always changing.

When we were still small she always said, when we lied, that we had a white cross on our foreheads. When we were big enough to look in the mirror and wanted to see the white cross, she told us that our ears **waggled** when we lied.

Flippi and I stood in front of the mirror and lied as hard as we could, but our ears never waggled.

Then our mother insisted that our legs would stop growing if we lied, and as proof she quoted the German saying: "Liars have short legs".

---

white lie – Notlüge; to waggle – wackeln

Later on I found out that the saying really goes: "Lies have short legs".

Finally my mother gave up, saying: "Lying isn't done, and that's the end of it!"

And much later she admitted that white lies are **permissible**. They were more or less OK. Not very nice, but sometimes very necessary.

She told me that when I caught her telling a friend on the phone that she had to hang up because there was someone at the door. I stood there and watched her run to the door with the phone in her hand, ring the doorbell and **cordially** welcomed someone who wasn't there at all. Never mind.

With a heavy heart I took BJ's jacket off again and handed it to Justus.

And Justus trotted off. I wanted to go with him, but Justus was a bit suspicious and said he'd rather settle the matter on his own.

Saturday afternoon, 27th June

Justus hasn't come back yet.

I'm sure BJ has discovered the bear's true powers and won't give him back. Justus and BJ will found a

---

permissible – zulässig; cordially – herzlich

witches' club and **compete** with each other in spell-making!

And I won't be a member. It's so unfair. After all, it's my bear!

Oskar spends almost every evening with us now. And that's really great. Oskar is truly all right.

He's almost cleaned up Flippi's room.

My mother usually helps him.

I think she wants to make a good **impression** on him. She doesn't shout at us any more. Nor does she ask us if we've got problems that she could help us solve.

And: she's bought herself a new blouse although she otherwise even sews our pencil cases herself. And she wears this blouse while she's painting. Well, that's something I'd never dare to do.

When Oskar wanted to make her a compliment, saying her new shirt looked good and that it was a pity to wear it for working, all she said was: "Oh, this old **rag**. I was going to sort it out anyway."

Then Oskar snipped off the price tag that was still **dangling** from the blouse and my mother blushed.

Oskar gave my mother such a sweet smile.

Flippi and I want Oskar to stay on, and we're

---

to compete – wetteifern; impression – Eindruck;
rag – Fetzen; to dangle – baumeln

already wondering which room to **wreck** next so that my mother will need Oskar for even longer. Because Flippi's room is nearly finished.

Flippi has also asked our mother whether we couldn't adopt Oskar. Then he would live with us and we would have a big brother. Oskar has lost both his parents and he lives all on his own.

My mother got a bit confused when Flippi made this **suggestion**. She said she wasn't very keen on the idea of an adoption. She thought it silly that the son should be older than the mother. He certainly wouldn't do what she told him.

Saturday evening, 27th June

Everything's OK. Justus has just been here.

With my bear. I nearly kissed him. Justus, I mean. But as we aren't in love with each other, I didn't do it, of course. That would only confuse Justus.

Instead, I kissed my bear.

Justus said he'd felt very embarrassed and told me to keep a closer eye on my lucky animals in future. BJ had nearly **rolled up with laughter** when Justus turned up in the role of the **saviour** of

---

to wreck – ruinieren; suggestion – Vorschlag; to roll up with laughter – sich ausschütten vor Lachen; saviour – Retter

children and cuddly toys, and had found the situation – and Justus – very funny.

I felt really sorry for Justus, but he hadn't wanted me to go with him. So it's his own fault. But I didn't say that, of course. You always have to praise boys, especially when they make mistakes.

I told him I thought it was really cool of him to do that for me.

That seemed to make Justus happy somehow. So happy that he asked me whether I'd like to go to the cinema with him.

I was so pleased to have my bear back that I said yes.

Now that I've got my bear back I can cast a spell to make BJ come to the cinema, too.

Because now that BJ has been walking around in my jacket for one entire day, he may well be in my power and have to do everything I ask of him.

Perhaps I'll get BJ to do my homework for me. And he'll have to take over my kitchen **chores** and clean the aquarium when it's my turn. And the rest of the time he'll have to kiss me and tell me that I'm the coolest girl he knows.

Flippi is still sharing my room. Flippi's room is only progressing very slowly.

Oskar finds it harder and harder **to get down to**

---

chore – Hausarbeit; to get down to work – zum Arbeiten kommen

work. He and my mother seem to have quite a lot to discuss, as Oskar is now supposed to decorate the other rooms, too. He had no objection when my mother asked him. On the contrary, he said no prob, any time. And since then they've been talking about the project. Mostly in her bedroom.

Maybe she only did it to prevent Flippi from running **artistically** amok again. Because Flippi came into the kitchen with her paintbox a few days ago and asked my mother whether she hadn't always wanted a little **border** of monsters around the walls. Flippi would love to paint it for her.

My mother jumped and told Flippi not to bother. She said she couldn't expect such a delicate little girl to work so hard. Flippi should enjoy her life, get together with the other girls and play. Preferably at their houses. She said she would ask Oskar to do a couple of sketches for a monster border which they could then discuss together.

Flippi was satisfied with her suggestion.

So now Oskar and my mother sit for hours in my mother's bedroom discussing the monster border.

---

artistically – künstlerisch; border – Bordüre

Tuesday, 30th June

Oskar really is a genius. Flippi's room is ready. He has transformed it into a super Flintstones cave. He's even painted Flintstones **furniture** on the wall. And he's painted Dino and Pebbles as well. And Fred and Wilma.

Flippi complained about these two, however. She said Fred and Wilma looked suspiciously like Oskar and our mother. Flippi's not so wrong. There they stand, hand in hand, and Wilma is **nuzzling up** to Fred like a real love-bird. And Oskar has painted hundreds of pink hearts around them, too.

When Flippi asked him what he meant by painting this piece of kitsch, Oskar got quite embarrassed. He said he had probably done it without thinking. Then he looked across at our mother. She stared down at the floor, drawing invisible circles with one foot.

Hey – wasn't that the sign for ...? Impossible! It must mean something quite different to adults.

---

furniture – Einrichtung; to nuzzle up – sich anschmiegen

Wednesday, 1st July

What a day today was! Incredible.

I went to the cinema with Justus. When he picked me up, he looked quite different from his usual self. It took me a while **to figure out** what it was: Justus had combed his hair. He never does that normally.

Actually, he always says he never combs his hair. But I expect it takes him at least an hour to make his hair look as coolly **tousled** and unkempt as it usually does.

Anyway, today he had a completely different hairstyle. One which looked combed. When I asked him, he shrugged his shoulders and said he looked just like he always did.

It was only on our way to the cinema that I remembered that I had really wanted to magic BJ to the cinema. But then I suddenly had the feeling that BJ might be in the way somehow. Nor did I really know how he would be in the way, or in the way of what. Anyway, I left BJ where he was.

At the cinema, Justus bought popcorn and Coke and found us seats quite a long way back in the corner.

When the lights went down, he stretched his arms up in the air and laid them on the seat backs

---

to figure out – herausfinden; tousled – zerzaust

on either side. But then a fat gentleman sat down next to Justus, so Justus quickly took that arm off the back of the seat. The one on the back of my seat he left where it was.

He asked me if I'd mind if he put his Coke on the other side of me.

I was very nice and said that sounded like a good idea, because the man sitting beside him looked pretty thirsty. He looked as if he might quite possibly take a **swig** of Justus's Coke.

Justus put his Coke beside me. Whenever he wanted to take a sip, which was quite often, he had to lean over me to get at the bottle. Each time he only took a teeny-weeny sip, but he took quite a lot of them.

I didn't know exactly what to do with my arms.

I wanted to be as cool as Justus, so I also put my arm on the back of the seat. At least I tried. But while I was trying, I knocked the popcorn out of Justus's hand. Then I stopped trying.

Justus said nothing.

Then I put my hand down by my Coke, which was between Justus and me.

Suddenly I felt something on my hand. I got such a shock because, in the film, there was a scene with a rat and I thought it was a rat. I **gave a shriek** and hectically pulled my hand away. Unfor-

---

swig – Schluck; to give a shriek – aufschreien

tunately, as I did so, I spilt my Coke over Justus's trousers.

Again, Justus said nothing.

I felt terribly embarrassed, especially when I noticed that it wasn't a rat but Justus's hand that had touched me.

Then Justus took his arm away from the back of my seat and stopped sipping his Coke, too.

I **clenched** my popcorn in both hands and felt a bit miserable. I thought it would be best to concentrate on the film.

It was a really exciting film. But when everything went dead quiet for just a second, we could hear someone noisily eating something and the sound of a spoon on a glass.

Justus turned round and then **nudged** me. "Look who's sitting in the row behind us."

I turned round and could hardly believe it. Who was sitting diagonally behind us? Klarafina. With an ice-cream sundae in her hand. She leaned over to me and said: "What a good thing we met, Jojo. I've something important to tell you."

I asked her if it couldn't wait till later but she said no, it had to be right now.

And because the people near us were already angrily clearing their throats and going "Shh!", I went out with Klarafina. Justus wanted to come with

---

to clench – umklammern; to nudge – anstupsen

us, but Klarafina pushed him back in his seat and whispered: "**Girl-talk**."

Klarafina and I then sat on the stairs. She took an ice-cream sundae for me and another for herself out of her handbag and said we had something important to discuss. But it was a very **tricky subject**. It had to do with boys.

I was afraid she was going to give me a **sex-talk** and told her I already knew all about it. My mother had given me a book about it when I was seven. And apart from that, we'd already learned everything a second time at school.

Klarafina was very surprised that 'witch ethics' was a school subject.

"Witch ethics?"

"Yes, the basic rules about what a witch may do and what she should under no circumstances do," explained Klarafina.

She seemed quite relieved when I told her that I had meant something quite different. No, I assured her, we hadn't had 'witch ethics' at school yet. Maybe we'll get it in the **sixth form**.

"That might be too late," said Klarafina.

"What's up?" I wanted to know.

Klarafina **hummed and hawed**. "Well," she began. "I have the feeling that you're about to

---

girl-talk – Frauensache; tricky subject – heikles Thema; sex-talk – Aufklärung; sixth form – Oberstufe; to hum and haw – herumdrucksen

break the most important of all witches' **commandments**."

"What's that? Going to the cinema? Eating popcorn? Spilling Coke?"

"No, no – it's got something to do with boys."

Well, of course I found that interesting. Anything to do with boys has interested me lately. "So what is it?"

Klarafina gave a deep sigh and took another big spoonful of ice-cream before replying.

It must have been very embarrassing for her, because she mumbled as unclearly as she could: "Mitches are mot for missing."

"What? Witches are not for missing?"

Klarafina shook her head, took a deep breath, and said in an even quieter but clearer voice: "Witches are not for kissing."

"Witches are not for kissing? I beg your pardon? What's that supposed to mean?"

"Exactly what I said. You have to **make your mind up**, Jojo. If you kiss or are kissed, you will lose your power as a witch."

"I don't believe you."

"But it's true."

"What sort of stupid commandment is that?"

"Everyone with a special gift has to make sacri-

---

commandment – Gebot;
to make up one's mind – sich entscheiden

fices. And witches are not allowed to kiss. Otherwise their witching days are over."

"No kissing – ever?"

"Never."

"Not even one teeny-weeny kisslet?"

"Not a single kiss."

"Till the end of my days?"

"Till the end of your days."

"So how do witches get children?"

"Witches don't get children. They seek out gifted girls and give them a special object with which they can cast spells. Only as long as they remain unkissed, of course."

Wow! How about that! I pointed to Mathilde, Klarafina nodded. So Mathilde is Klarafina's bear, so to speak.

The film was over. Justus came out to us. I was just going to suggest that we should go to the ice-cream parlour, but Klarafina **scurried** off.

Instead, Serafina was suddenly standing beside us. Justus asked her how she had enjoyed the film. She said the film had been boring, but she found what was going on out here all the more interesting. And as she walked past me, she whispered: "Best regards to your friend."

No idea what she meant by that.

---

to scurry – huschen

All the way home the words were echoing in my ears: 'Witches are not for kissing, witches are not for kissing, witches are not for kissing …'

And Justus, walking beside me, was talking and talking and talking. I think he was telling me how the film ended. But I couldn't have cared less how the film ended. I'm wondering how my life will end.

When we reached our front door, Justus put his arm around me. I gave a terrified shriek because I thought he was going to kiss me. Justus was also startled and asked me what was the matter with me.

I was so frightened that I said: "Witches are not for kissing."

Justus rolled his eyes and said I had probably eaten too much popcorn.

Yes, that must be it, I said to him. A doctor had once discovered that popcorn has a **narcotic** effect on me. I really shouldn't touch the stuff at all. Like **poppy-seed rolls** – one bite and I'm high!

Justus smiled weakly and said he had to go home now.

I was really happy to be alone. I have to make an important decision.

I mean, just think: think what I've been working towards all these weeks! My life ruined! I can't

---

narcotic – berauschen; poppy-seed rolls – Mohnbrötchen

believe it!! And the number of times I've missed being kissed **by a hair's breadth**? At least two near misses with BJ.

Probably I ought even to be thankful to Flippi. What a piece of luck.

What do I mean: 'What a piece of luck'? I can never kiss BJ. What else am I living for? What a stupid situation! And I had been so much looking forward to my first kiss!

But there can be no question of my giving up my magic powers. Certainly not now that everything in my life is going in the right direction at last. Well, *almost* everything.

Everybody wishes he or she could do magic, and I can do it.

I certainly won't risk that for a stupid old kiss.

That's right. What's so special about BJ anyway that would make anybody want to kiss him **at all costs**?

There's nothing special about BJ at all.

The best thing will be to keep away from boys completely, then nothing can possibly go wrong.

But suddenly I had to think about Justus. And I began to cry.

I can't understand it: I'm in love with BJ, and

---

by a hair's breadth – um Haaresbreite;
at all costs – unbedingt

when I think about Justus, I have to start **blubbing**.

Maybe it's because it's somehow more fun to do things with Justus. Not only because he's nicer than BJ. Justus is also funnier. Actually, BJ is only cool and nothing else.

Oh, no! Maybe I've fallen in love with the wrong boy. Just my bad luck! Something like that could only happen to me! That I think the boy I've fallen in love with is not as nice as the one I'm not in love with.

That must be puberty. Maybe I'll catch it after all.

So, one thing is clear: I shall never kiss. I shall remain a witch!

Yes, a witch is what I'll be.

Thursday, 2nd July

Justus is **avoiding me**.

And all the other boys at school are **chasing me** like crazy. Their behaviour is absolutely dotty. They've probably all gone nuts or something. Have they all caught puberty at the same time?

Manuel came up to me during break, put his arm

---

to blub – flennen; to avoid sb – jmd. aus dem Weg gehen; to chase sb – jmd. hinterherrennen

round my shoulders and whispered: "Hello, Jojo." And he tried to kiss me. Seriously!

I jumped aside in horror, bumping into Torsten – then *he* tried to kiss me! I punched him in the eye and slapped Manuel round the face because he was still standing there and making a face as if he was going to try again.

Then they both walked over to Serafina and told her that I was a stupid little bitch.

Two boys from Eighth Grade also went up to Serafina, looked across at me and asked her: "Is that the one?"

Serafina nodded, and the two of them walked up to me. One of them asked: "Hey, are you Jojo? Cool! Do you want go to the cinema with me?"

The other one pushed his friend aside and said he was there first. Then the two of them started arguing, and I **buzzed off**.

Then Serafina walked over to the boys and called them two stupid twits. I think it's great if boys are crazy about you, but Serafina is behind it somehow so I don't have a good feeling.

When I told Linda everything, she said that might be a good sign and that Serafina might perhaps want me to join her club soon when she sees how **popular** I suddenly am.

Well, Linda might just be right.

---

to buzz off – die Fliege machen; popular – beliebt

Monday, 6th July

At last!

I'm one of the cool kids. Oh, I knew it all the time!

Serafina came up to me today and was as friendly as can be. She asked me whether I wouldn't like to be a member of her club.

At last.

"Of course," I said.

"OK," was her reply. "Then you are accepted herewith."

Of course there was just one little thing, naturally. Really only a **trifle**.

"What is it? Tell me what it is and I'll do it."

"Well," she went on, "every new member of the club has to hand over an old cuddly toy at the start. As an indication that they aren't a baby any longer, **so to speak**, and are prepared to give up their favourite cuddly animal."

"No prob. I've got an old dog with blue button eyes, a monkey with **Velcro** paws who can really cling to you or a sweet little kangaroo. Which one would you like?"

"Your bear!"

"My bear?!"

---

trifle – Kleinigkeit; so to speak – sozusagen;
Velcro – Klettverschluss

"That's right."

The shock made me feel quite sick. Why does she want my bear? My bear of all things?

Thank God the bell for the next lesson rang. I buried the bear deep in my pocket and said I didn't have him with me today. I said I'd bring him along tomorrow.

Serafina smiled in triumph.

Tuesday, 7th July

I couldn't sleep all night.

I'm so unhappy about my bear. I simply can't give my bear away.

What on earth can I do? Here's my **one-time** chance to be one of the 'in kids', but to be one of them I have to give up my bear. Anything else but my bear – giving him away would mean that I wouldn't be able to do magic anymore.

But perhaps you have to make sacrifices if you want something **badly** enough.

---

one-time – einmalig; badly – dringend

Tuesday evening, 7th July

The strangest thing in the world happened today.

Serafina came up to me and asked me if I'd brought the bear. I put on my most rueful face and said I'd forgotten him. In order to gain time. Because I'm still not quite sure whether I should really give him away.

Serafina was a bit cross and told me she wouldn't **keep her offer open** much longer.

Then the following happened: BJ and a couple of other boys were standing around and whispering among themselves. Yes, even boys whisper. And how!

Then BJ said to the boys: "That's **money for old rope**!"

He strolled up to Serafina and me, swept Serafina into his arms and kissed her.

I was completely gobsmacked. I waited for my heart to break. But nothing happened. I mean it's a bit funny, isn't it? The boy I'm in love with kisses my **arch enemy** and I feel nothing.

Why did he kiss Serafina anyway? Just like that – in front of all the others?

I'm sure he must have lost a bet. He wouldn't do a thing like that **voluntarily**, I thought.

---

to keep an offer open – ein Angebot aufrechterhalten; money for old rope – leicht verdientes Geld; arch enemy – Erzfeindin; voluntarily – freiwillig

But then things got even better: BJ finishes his kiss, holds out his hand demandingly and says: "OK. That was that. Now give me my twenty Euros."

"What?! You have to pay BJ twenty Euros for one kiss?"

Well, how lucky I am that BJ and I haven't got around to kissing yet, otherwise I'd be **stony broke** already.

Nor did Serafina seem to be very happy about it either, because she slapped BJ round the ears and screamed at him: "Not *me*, you stupid twit! *Her!*" And when she said 'her' she pointed to *me*.

"Oh," said BJ. "A little misunderstanding." He was just about to grab me when Serafina slapped him round the face again and screamed that he had ruined her life.

She began to cry **heartrendingly**, and BJ asked her what was wrong now. Was he supposed to kiss me or wasn't he?

But Serafina ran off, and I clenched my fists, took up a fighting position and **snarled at** BJ: "Don't you dare!"

BJ shrugged his shoulders and walked away.

And suddenly everything was crystal clear to me.

That rotten, scheming little bitch had offered the

---

stony broke – völlig pleite; heartrendingly – herzzerreißend; to snarl at sb – jmd. anblaffen

boys at school money to kiss me! Serafina must have been **eavesdropping** on my conversation with Klarafina at the cinema. She wanted me to lose my magic powers and she wanted my bear.

Good heaven! And I nearly fell for it!

But I'm sure of one thing now. I'm not in love with BJ, I know that for certain. It's all over between BJ and me.

It's just a pity that Justus is keeping out of my way. He hasn't phoned me since our cinema fiasco. And if we see each other in the school playground and I say 'Hi' to him, he only gives me the briefest of greetings and walks on.

Wednesday afternoon, 8th July

I can't believe it. It simply can't be true.

I come home. Everything is quiet. I think that there's nobody at home and want to see how the monster border in the kitchen is coming along. I walk into the kitchen and what do I see???

My mother and Oskar! Kissing each other!!!

I must have screamed with fright, because the two of them immediately stopped what they were

---

to eavesdrop – belauschen

doing. They rushed across to me and tried to calm me down, constantly asking me what the matter was.

At first I couldn't say a word. But then I found myself **hissing at** the two of them, asking them just what they thought they were doing. I told them they weren't teenagers any more, and that kissing would cost them their magic powers.

I must have been a bit confused, because my mother put me to bed. She sat beside me for hours, put a wet **facecloth** on my forehead and kept forcing me to drink camomile tea.

I cried rather a lot and told her how rotten it was that my mother should be allowed to kiss and that I wasn't.

My mother was very kind to me, so somehow I told her everything – about BJ and Justus and so on.

She asked me whether I might not **actually** be in love with Justus.

I denied it. Nobody was in love with Justus, I said. Except perhaps Linda, but she falls in love with a different guy each week. Justus isn't exactly one of the cool boys. Those were BJ and the **blokes** in the band. They were the ones you fell in love with if you wanted to be cool.

My mother told me to get some rest, and went

---

to hiss at sb – jmd. anfauchen; facecloth – Waschlappen; actually – in Wirklichkeit; bloke – Typ

back to her darling. Yes, she's the lucky one! She's in love and can kiss as much as she likes.

While I was resting, I thought the whole thing through again carefully and came to the conclusion that you might possibly fall in love without actually wanting to. Just like that. You meet someone, find him attractive and whoops! Suddenly you're in love. Whether you like it or not.

And that might have happened to me with Justus.

So I might actually be in love with Justus and not with BJ. Otherwise my heart would have broken when BJ kissed Serafina. That's what it says in all the novels: 'When she saw him with the other woman, her heart broke.'

The fact that I'm always so nervous and that embarrassing things happen to me when I'm with Justus might be a sign of love.

And the tickling I feel in my tummy isn't an allergy – it's love.

All the signs are that I'm in love with Justus. And now I have to tell him that we have no future because **otherwise** I would lose my powers as a witch!

Unless, of course, he promises never to kiss me.

If he really loves me, he'll do that!

Suddenly I realized that I don't really know whether Justus is in love with me anyway. I never

---

otherwise – anderenfalls

paid much attention to him because I always had only eyes for BJ.

Suddenly I burst out crying again. Because if Justus isn't in love with me, our love story would be a really sad one.

Wednesday evening, 8th July

I don't like to admit it, but I asked my mother how I can find out whether Justus loves me or not.

For heaven's sake, I must be really **desperate** to ask my own mother for advice!

But she's probably better informed in love matters than I had always thought.

Well, at least she said she was sure that Justus thought I was **fantastic**. Anyone who sacrifices so much of his free time to be with me as Justus has simply must find me fantastic.

She was really nice and almost normal, and this was the first time that she didn't reproach herself for having done everything wrong. Nor did she blame my father.

So, if Justus also loves *me*, I only have to decide what to do about this kissing nonsense.

Shall I kiss Justus or not?

---

desperate – verzweifelt; fantastic – toll

If I want to kiss Justus, I shall simply kiss him! What do I need the powers of a witch for? It's much more important in life to be kissed.

Tomorrow I will kiss Justus!

Thursday, 9th July

This morning I was able to think clearly again, and made a new decision:

I *won't* kiss Justus.
I want to remain a witch.

I talked to Justus in the school playground during break.

I explained to him that I was in love with him and was prepared to marry him, but that I would **unfortunately** never be able to kiss him.

Justus was rather **taken aback**, but told me that was OK. We could just go to the cinema now and then **for starters**, and perhaps to a concert or to a basketball match occasionally.

I told him that was OK by me. That would be all right.

---

unfortunately – bedauerlicherweise; to be taken aback – verblüfft sein; for starters – für den Anfang

Thank goodness he didn't ask for any explanations.

He already thinks I'm a bit peculiar in any case, and all my explanations only seem to confuse him.

Oh, he was so-o-o sweet!

But then something terrible happened.

Well, actually it wasn't terrible at all.

I had just finished my flaming speech when Justus gave me a loving glance, rather like the way Oskar looks at my mother. And then it happened.

I kissed Justus.

I kissed him! Although I'm not allowed to kiss at all!

And that was the most fantastic feeling I've ever had in my life.

I'm totally happy. And so is Justus. And I **don't give a damn** that I can't cast spells any more.

So what shall I do with the bear now?

I could give him to Serafina.

Then she'll let me join her club. And as she is no longer unkissed, she won't be able to do any evil spells with him.

---

not to give a damn – sich nichts daraus machen

Friday, 10th July

So, everything's hunky-dory now: I've given the bear away.

It wasn't easy for me. But I can see him every day. And he wouldn't work for me any more anyway.

I definitely made the right decision.

Flippi was ever so pleased.

Yes, Flippi! I gave the bear to my little sister!

Not to Serafina, that conceited old cow! She can stick her silly club wherever she likes.

I'm an adult now.

Justus will be **picking me up** soon. We're going for a picnic.

And last night something else wonderful happened. I got my first pimple! It looks rather sweet actually. Right next to my nose. I shall call him Pünktchen. And if I get another pimple, I shall call him Anton. I'll call the next one … Oh, I don't think I should think about that so much. I don't need a lot of pimples. One or two will do fine.

Flippi wanted to cast a spell on Oskar and our mother so that they would get married. But I told her we'd give them a chance and see if it didn't **happen of its own accord**. We'll give those two a week.

---

to pick sb up – jmd. abholen; to happen of its own accord – von selbst geschehen

If they haven't got married by then, Flippi will start casting her spells.

Tomorrow I'm meeting Klarafina, and I'll introduce her to Flippi. As my **successor**, so to speak.

There's no danger of Flippi kissing a boy. The most Flippi does is to punch boys in the stomach.

She thinks boys are absolutely stupid.

At the moment.

And Flippi told me that if ever I have a big wish, she'll magic it into **fulfilment**.

But it may well be that I don't need magic any more. Because if you really want something to work out, you can do it without witchcraft. You only have to want it hard enough.

Well, and sometimes things work out that you don't want, but which turn out to be much better than what you wanted in the first place.

And if you get annoyed about all the things you want and don't get, then you should remember that there are still heaps of things that you *don't* want which fortunately you don't get, either.

That sounds a bit mixed up again, doesn't it? But that's all because of puberty. I'm certain that I've caught it now.

---

successor – Nachfolger; fulfilment – Erfüllung

Von Hortense Ullrich bereits erschienen:

Hexen küsst man nicht (1)
Liebeskummer lohnt sich (2)
Doppelt geküsst hält besser (3)
Liebe macht blond (4)
Love is Blonde
Wer zuletzt küsst … (5)
Und wer liebt mich? (6)
And Who Loves Me?
Ein Kuss kommt selten allein (7)
Unverhofft liebt oft (8)
Ehrlich küsst am längsten (9)
Andere Länder, andere Küsse (10)
Kein Tanz, kein Kuss (11)
Liebe auf den ersten Kuss (12)
Kuss oder Schluss (13)
Ohne Chaos keine Küsse (14)
Chaosküsse mit Croissant (15)
Verküsst noch mal (16)
Neuer Kuss, neues Glück (17)
Ketchup, Kuss und Kaviar (18)

Ullrich, Hortense
Never Kiss a Witch
Aus dem Deutschen von Philip und Regine Hewitt
ISBN 978 3 522 50138 5

Reihen- und Einbandgestaltung: Birgit Schössow
Texttypografie: Marlis Killermann
Schrift: New Baskerville
Satz: KCS GmbH in Buchholz/Hamburg
Reproduktion: Medienfabrik, Stuttgart
Druck und Bindung: Friedrich Pustet, Regensburg

Die deutsche Originalausgabe erschien
unter dem Titel *Hexen küsst man nicht.*
Printed in Germany.
6 5 4 3 2* 12 13 14 15

Freche Mädchen – freche Bücher!

von Hortense Ullrich

1 – Hexen küsst man nicht
ISBN 978 3 522 50117 0

2 – Liebeskummer lohnt sich
ISBN 978 3 522 50039 5

3 – Doppelt geküsst hält besser
ISBN 978 3 522 50041 8

4 – Liebe macht blond

ISBN 978 3 522 50052 4

5 – Wer zuletzt küsst ...

ISBN 978 3 522 50053 1

6 – ... und wer liebt mich?
ISBN 978 3 522 50024 1

7 – Ein Kuss kommt selten allein
ISBN 978 3 522 50105 7

8 – Unverhofft liebt oft

ISBN 978 3 522 50047 0

9 – Ehrlich küsst am längsten
ISBN 978 3 522 50025 8